Buddy Bolden
and the
Last Days of Storyville

by
Danny Barker

edited by Alyn Shipton

CASSELL
London and New York

Cassell
Wellington House, 125 Strand, London WC2R 0BB
370 Lexington Avenue, New York, NY 10017-6550

First published in Great Britain in 1998 by Cassell by arrangement with Bayou Press Ltd

British Library Cataloguing-in-Publication Data
A catalogue record for this book is available from the British Library.

ISBN 0-304-70106-8 (hardback)

Library of Congress Cataloging-in-Publication Data
Barker, Danny
    Buddy Bolden and the last days of Storyville / by Danny Barker;
edited by Alyn Shipton.
        p.   cm.
    Includes index.
    ISBN 0-304-70106-8 (hardback)
        1. Jazz—Louisiana—New Orleans—History and criticism.
    I. Shipton, Alyn.   II. Title.
    ML3508.8.N48B37   1998
    781.65'09763'35—dc21   98–12250
                                                                    CIP
                                                                    MN

Typeset by Oompah Books, Wheatley
Printed and bound in Great Britain by Biddles Ltd, Guildford and King's Lynn

Contents

The publication of this book has been made possible by a Peter Whittingham Award administered by the Musicians' Benevolent Fund.

Editor's Note

The idea of Buddy Bolden and his importance as "the first man of jazz" was one which preoccupied Danny Barker and influenced much of his writing and research over more than four decades. This tale and the dying days of Storyville were themes that regularly recurred in his writing and conversation, and when we agreed to collaborate on his autobiography *A Life In Jazz* it was always with the intention that his writings on jazz's infancy and early social environment would be collected and published separately. I regret that Danny did not live to see this task completed, but in this book I have attempted to bring together his finished pieces in the form we had planned together, and I am grateful to his widow Blue Lu Barker and his daughter Sylvia for all their help in achieving this. Central to the whole project was Danny's outspoken and honest view of the racial climate in which he had grown up. He wrote one half-finished piece on why the social mores of the South had contributed to Bolden's insanity, and he clearly identified with the idea that a musician might be driven insane by prejudice. One section of that piece reads:

> "In New Orleans [the Negro] soon observes that the only places his people can express themselves loudly and without restraint or caution are at Protestant churches, dances, parades and games of sport. Never at political rallies or civic affairs because his folks rarely attend such affairs other than as servants and caretakers.
>
> In my case I learned early that I would never see the inside of a college. I also found out that if I wanted to go places with a minimum of education, the way involved the learning of a musical instrument – that is, if you could play like King Oliver, Bunk Johnson, Sidney Bechet, Bud Scott or Kid Ory, the public did not ask if you could read or write or count. Also I saw and heard that a great musician was welcome anywhere – in honky tonks or in kings' castles. The word had reached New Orleans that Freddie Keppard was up north with his Creole Band, playing in the biggest theaters; that Mamie Smith was making phonograph records; Sidney Bechet had played for the King of England inside the palace and New Orleans musicians were leaving every week, going to all parts of the United States and sending reports of how nicely they

were treated by the people up north. They would send back books, magazines, newspaper clippings, pictures of the fine places where they played. I saw that the lowest jobs were done by Negroes and they never were promoted. So my mind was set on one thing: learn to play something.

When I was a small boy I got to figuring about what a predicament I was in – that is, being a Negro (American style). That is American Negro – American citizen. Thinking of the many things I was compelled to do in a certain special fashion and pattern (Southern style) led me to realize that I had to be two people: An American citizen first and an American Negro always and that if I curved or deviated from the set pattern I would definitely get into a lot of trouble as many Negroes had done before.

So I began to ask questions of the older folks. I asked so many questions till I got tired and I just followed the crowd. . . Now, concerning Buddy Bolden's insanity – one of the main contributing factors which led to his mental collapse is the Great White South's Perpetual Proclamation: 'Ouah Way of Life.'

There are many hundreds of people I have been in close contact with who are considered to be sound and sane but in my opinion these people should be confined to institutions. Many public figures are permitted to roam about and do all sorts of idiotic things and they get away with such behavior."

Danny's concept of Buddy Bolden is one born of folklore, and a folklore promulgated by the musicians that Danny himself knew and played with, including Bunk Johnson and Jelly Roll Morton. Research in the 1970s by Donald M. Marquis has shown that much of Johnson and Morton's colorful accounts was hearsay, and that it is unlikely Bolden was ever a barber, a scandalsheet publisher or the owner of a shop. We do know that Bolden was a plasterer and that he worked for an Albert Poree, but there is no established connection between this Mr. Poree and the proprietor of Lincoln Park in Danny's tale. We also know from Bolden's widow that her husband "drank a lot and hung out at barber shops," while one of his lifelong friends was the barber Louis Jones from his home neighborhood.

Despite such scholarly detective work, what Danny has given his readers from the stories told to him by many musicians over several decades, is a living, breathing portrait of the Bolden first characterised by

Editor's Note

Bunk Johnson. Marquis speculates that Johnson misled Bill Russell and other researchers (including Danny) because of "his bitterness at being overlooked for years." Yet if some of the vital ingredients of the Bolden myth do turn out to be hearsay promoted by Bunk and his followers, much of the rest of Mr. Dude Bottley's account can be proven.

For a start, Buddy Bottley (or Bartley) was a real figure, the "colored aeronaut" who made "astonishing, perplexing, fascinating" ascents by balloon, advertised regularly in the New Orleans *Item* in 1905. The other aspects of Lincoln Park entertainments are verifiable from contemporary press reports and the testimony of many elderly musicians interviewed for the Tulane archives. Equally the Bolden / Pickett *contre-temps* happened, Mrs. Susanna Pickett telling Donald Marquis in 1971 that her husband "mentioned that Buddy thought everyone was his enemy and was out to get him." Manuel "Fess" Manetta recalled Bolden appearing with Henry Allen Sr.'s Brass Band, although it is reasonably certain that Bolden's last parade was downtown in New Orleans and not across the river.

A Memory of King Bolden is greatly expanded from the form in which it was originally published in *Evergreen Review* in September 1965, with an introduction by the late Martin Williams. As with *A Life In Jazz*, I am grateful to Martin, to Nat Hentoff and Donald Phelps for giving their permission to reuse material first published under their aegis. Danny wrote and rewrote this story several times, and I have worked from the most complete draft, which included several new sections to be inserted and copious handwritten notes. The original did not include the story of the greasy pig and the balloon, both of which create a marvelous feeling of the atmosphere of Lincoln Park. The first published version ends with Dude Bottley listening to Buddy Bolden playing the song that alternates between church music and the blues. It made a dramatic end, but Danny's newer sections on the parade and Bolden's committal are essential components of his version of the Bolden myth. When I asked him outright about whether Dude Bottley was real, or a figment of his imagination, Danny gave me one of his quizzical looks. Of course, he said, when he gave the original draft to Martin Williams, he'd added "a little monkeyshine," but the story was in essence true, and he had put it together from many accounts collected over the years.

Even so, there are a few loose ends that I have left untouched. The Piccard twins, for example, were in fact Swiss, and their main exploits took place in the field of balloon research quite a few years after Bolden was committed to Jackson, Louisiana. It is highly unlikely that a character like Mr. Poree was running a motor car quite as early as this. Also, Danny has telescoped time between Dusen firing Bolden from the band, Buddy's last parade and his committal, condensing events that took place between September 1906 and June 1907 into a few days.

ix

Editor's Note

There is a particular irony in the setting of the Dude Bottley story as an oral history interview, which is another part of the piece also omitted from the originally published version. One of the things Danny felt very strongly, and which came out in our discussions and correspondence about this book, was that those who write on jazz and jazz-related subjects ought to have paid their dues in knowing about the subject. Few people in jazz history knew their subject better, and yet it took many years for the first pieces of Danny's fine, colorful and informed writing about jazz to be published, while other, lesser writers were seemingly able to rush plenty of mis-information into print. Danny was a pioneer of African American research, being one of the first jazz musicians to interview or send questionnaires to his subjects, as he says in the *Houses of Ill Repute* chapter. Dude Bottley is tacitly giving us Danny's own views when he says: "I'm so glad to see that some Negro is interested in writing a story so that the people will remember the great Bolden and Lincoln Park, and what the good old days were like."

I will come on to the subject of Danny's copious research among the generation of jazz musicians that preceded his own, but almost all today's researchers who have investigated Storyville and its characters (many of whose names are only otherwise known to us as one-line references in the Police department's arrest files for the period) will already know how Danny's memories and lists of personalities have enriched the resources at Tulane's William Ransome Hogan Jazz Archive, the Amistad Research Center and the Louisiana State Museum. I have consulted all the holdings on Danny in these institutions, and in April 1987 interviewed him about many of the names he recalled. Material from all these sources has been integrated into *The Last Days of Storyville* and the other chapters concerning the District. I am grateful to Bruce Boyd Raeburn and Alma D. Williams at the Jazz Archive, Rebecca Hankins at the Amistad Research Center and Steven D. Teeter at the State Museum for their help.

The Last Days of Storyville is a composite of several of Danny's tales, but its overall form was set out in a typescript which Danny handed to me as we started this project. It provided a context for his shorter set-pieces on Clerk Wade and Whitefolks Weber. There are three different extant endings to the Clerk Wade story, each with minor differences in language and detail, but the version that appears here is the one Danny himself selected for the composite story. The tale of Wade is a well-known piece of New Orleans folklore, and a version of it appears in Louis Armstrong's memoirs and is reprinted in Laurence Bergreen's 1997 biography of Armstrong. As atmospheric as Armstrong's version is, Danny manages to recreate the characters involved with the skill of a master storyteller.

Editor's Note

The rest of the book moves gradually forward in time. Even when the setting is at a later date, often it is still the District and its characters who are recalled, by the oral memories of Bottley, from the tales at "Cookshop's", by Pops Foster, by Danny himself or by Hamp Benson and George Baquet. Each chapter draws together miniatures that Danny had prepared for eventual inclusion in this book. The book ends in New York, at the time Danny was a member of the Cab Calloway band, with its acute portrait of the musicians' underworld of the "smoke dens." I am grateful to Karen Mix at the Mugar Memorial Library in Boston for access to the Cab Calloway Collection, where I discovered just how famous and well-respected a figure Danny became during his time with Cab, and where I was able to discover some rich and vivid pictures of his work in that band.

The crux of this book is to be found in the *Houses Of Ill Repute* chapter. In it, Danny explains for the first time in print about his extraordinary one-man research operation. Sections of his surviving questionnaires and from Hamp Benson's correspondence are reproduced in the plate section. (I have preserved Hamp's words in the text as they appeared in his letter, but have added in parentheses the correct names of some of the characters he refers to.) Research of this type has been done all too seldom in jazz, and almost never in a context independent of academic institutions or lexicographical requirements. If Danny's efforts had been properly recognized during the 1940s when he was in contact with the first generation of jazzmen, our knowledge of early jazz might be even richer. As it is, this book gives an insight into the lives of the Storyville generation at a depth that has rarely found its way into print, backed up by more complex research than simply a talent for storytelling and folk memory. Danny, of course, had both these talents in abundance, and I am glad that at least one consequence of the publication of *A Life In Jazz* was that his remarkable gifts as a raconteur found a larger audience, and that among his copious awards (too numerous to be listed here) many of them drew attention to this aspect of Danny's legacy.

Perhaps the most concise memorial to this remarkable man is the wording of the plaque that has been erected on his birthplace at 1027 Chartres Street: "African American Creole guitar and banjo player, songwriter, singer, author, historian, teacher, storyteller, humorist, actor and painter. Jazz Hall of Fame member, Recipient of National Endowment of the Arts Music Master Award and numerous other honors. Played on over 1,000 records of Jazz, Swing, Blues, Bebop and Traditional. Husband of legendary singer Blue Lu Barker."

Alyn Shipton
Oxford, England
January 1998

1
A Memory of King Bolden

While in New Orleans in 1955, I was searching out the few old-time musicians who had known and seen Buddy Bolden. I asked many questions, but few of them could recall any personal experiences with Bolden. I was telling my problem to a group of younger musicians, friends of mine, when Manuel Sayles said, "I know somebody who knew Buddy Bolden. He'll burn your ears off, telling about Bolden and Lincoln Park."

I said, "Who is it?"

Sayles said, "He is old Mr. Dude Bottley. His brother was Buddy Bottley who used to promote the dances at Lincoln Park. I'll see him for you. He'll be glad to tell you about Bolden."

Mr. Dude Bottley was living with his niece, a daughter of his brother Buddy Bottley. When Manny Sayles told me about his old neighbor, who lived just next door to him and was always talking about the old days, I asked, "Does he know what he is talking about or does he just talk to be talking?"

Sayles, a wonderful guitar and banjo player, who I studied with when I first started to play music, said, "Sure he knows what he is talking about and if you want to get some real facts about Buddy Bolden and what Lincoln Park was like he'll tell you all about it. Sometimes in the evening when I'm not busy and I feel like getting some laughs, I go to the front of my house and see if Mr. Dude is sitting on his porch. Generally he can be found there with maybe three or four other old men. They talk and argue and tell all kinds of stories about the olden days.

"When I see them out on the porch I go over and listen. If they are playing checkers I don't go because they will be quiet, nobody saying nothing, just playing and watching the game. If they are in a talking mood I go over and after a while I start asking them all kinds of questions. They will tell you about anything that happened in New Orleans after the Civil War. All I do is just mention somebody's name, or something that happened, and that starts them off. They'll get to arguing about who did this

1

or who did that until old Mr. Dude says: 'Now wait, gentlemen, that ain't the way it happened. This is what caused the whole thing.' "

I asked Sayles if he could arrange for me to meet Dude Bottley. Sayles said, "Sure I'll speak to him and call you. You bring your tape recorder and start asking him questions."

"How old is he?" I asked.

Sayles replied, "I'm sure he is way up in the seventies."

A couple of days later, Sayles called me. I went uptown to his house, and together we went next door to the home of Mr. Dude's niece. Sayles introduced me to Mr. Dude and his niece and we sat in the parlor, which was a large neat room, very clean and airy. His niece smiled and said, "Make yourselves at home."

Mr. Dude, Sayles and I relaxed, and I told Mr. Dude that I was gathering historical material for a jazz book. I opened the tape recorder.

He had never before seen or heard of one. Sayles and I located an outlet and plugged the wire in. Mr. Dude watched us very closely as I spoke into the mike and then played my voice back. He smiled and said, "Son, what is that machine called?"

"A tape recorder," I said, and handed him the mike for him to speak into. I played his voice back for him and he shook his head and laughed.

"What these white folks gonna invent next? This contraption will send a man straight to the penitentiary!"

His niece, who was standing in the doorway watching and laughing at the surprised reaction of her uncle, asked, "Where is his voice coming from? Is it on a record?"

So I explained the tape to them. She shook her head in surprise, and went to the rear, returning with a tray of glasses and beer. She placed the tray on a table and laughed, "There will be some long talking here this evening. How long does a tape run?"

I said, "About and hour and a half."

She asked, "How much a tape cost?"

"Three dollars"

She counted on her fingers and said, "You'll need about

one hundred tapes."

I said, surprised, "No, just three or four."

"No, sir, mister! When uncle really gets down to talking you gonna need a wagon load of them tapes. You don't know my uncle. When he starts to really talking, you'll be here 'til tomorrow this time."

We all laughed, and Mr. Dude said, pretending to be annoyed, "That's not nice to say that!" Then, holding the mike to his mouth, smiling with his eyes all lit up, he said, "Now, what you want me to talk about?"

I said, "I would like to know what kind of a person Buddy Bolden was. What happened in Lincoln Park? Tell me something about your brother, Buddy Bottley. Tell me of Frankie Dusen. Who owned Lincoln Park? Tell me about the musicians in Bolden's band. Why did Bolden lose his mind? What was the atmosphere of Lincoln Park? What kind of music did Bolden play? What type of people came to the park? Just tell me some of the things you saw happen around the band and the park."

Mr. Dude said, "That's just as easy as eating pie. My bones are old, but my mind is young and I can picture everything I saw just like if it happened yesterday."

By this time I had seen enough to agree that he was old in his bones but not in his mind. His senses were sharp, though he was slow in his movements, and he suffered none of the infirmities of old age. He did not chain smoke or inhale deeply on his pipe. He'd light it, take a couple of puffs and let it go out. When Sayles and I arrived, Mr. Bottley had the *Times Picayune* in his hand, folded to the editorial page. This paper is New Orleans' conservative newspaper: "The Voice of the South."

I turned the recorder on, and Dude Bottley said, "What's your name, son."

"Danny."

He said, "Dan, turn off that contraption for a minute, so we can put things I am going to say right. First, is it all right if I tell something about the beginnings of Lincoln Park and the conditions in those days?

I said, "Sure, anything you want to tell about that you

3

remember."

He said, "If what I am gonna tell you about is to be printed in a book, you will need the facts. I have a book around this house somewhere that is related about Winin' Boy, you know, Jelly Roll. My niece saw the book downtown and brought it to me to read. It is a good book, and I enjoyed reading it very much."

I was surprised. I said, "Did you know Jelly Roll?"

He replied, "I sure did. He lived in this neighborhood when he was a youngster. He and my brother were good pals. That Winin' Boy could do some talking. My brother used to call him Loudmouth. Reading that book was just like hearing him talk in person."

I said, "Well, that's the idea. You just speak like Jelly Roll."

He said, "You know, music is a wonderful subject and I started to take up the trombone but I never got around to buying one. I almost bought one, but I didn't because I used to see the men in Bolden's band get paid and that money was too measly for all that preparation a musician has to go through. I sat down and figured the whole music situation out. Musicians do not get the pay they deserve for all the pleasure they give people.

"Now turn on that contraption," he continued, "and I'll start talking."

I turned the lever, and he began to talk. As Mr. Bottley spoke, I learned that he was fairly educated and well-informed about life. After he had talked for about twenty minutes there was a light knock on the front door. I turned off the recorder, and Sayles opened the door. Mr. Dude smiled when he saw his guests, two old men, standing at the door.

"Come in, gentlemen," he greeted them. As they entered the room, Mr. Dude winked to me slyly and with a mischievous expression he put his finger to his lips. His actions meant: "Don't let on to nothin', let's see their surprised behavior."

When the two elderly men had removed their hats, Mr. Dude said pleasantly, smiling and pointing to the sofa, "Have a seat, gentlemen."

The visitors slowly and carefully walked across the wires and tapes and seated themselves, just looking at everything at once, suspicious and surprised. Mr. Dude winked at me again and said: "Dan, turn on the recorder." Which I did. I could hardly keep from laughing at the bewildered expression on the men's faces. They just sat silently, looking very carefully, intent on not moving or making a sound.

Mr. Dude spoke into the mike, enunciating very carefully: "As I was saying before I was suddenly interrupted, the Government of the United States of America has sent Mr. Dan to record my voice as I tell the great historical story of Buddy Bolden and Lincoln Park. The Government sent Dan from way up north in the capital, Washington, D.C., at great expense of taxpayers' money, to get this famous story." He paused, turned to me and said, "Mr. Dan, will you kindly play that portion of my great speech back, so we may detect if there are any flaws in it?"

His niece, who was standing in the doorway, laughed. The two old men looked at her, surprised, and then at Dude, the tape, me and Sayles. They didn't know what to think. They just looked about dumbfounded.

When the tape repeated Mr. Dude's voice, I turned it up loud and clear. They looked at each other, pop-eyed. Still no-one said a word. Everybody went along with the mystery. Mr. Dude continued talking and he didn't offer a word of explanation to the two men who sat there mystified at the proceedings.

After about ten minutes of this, they hunched one another, and one of them said, very apologetically and very softly, "We're leaving."

I motioned to Mr. Dude to continue his narration; Sayles opened the door and they very carefully and quietly walked through the doorway and left the house. Sayles lingered at the door, laughing as he watched the actions of the men on the outside. Then he returned to sit next to me, laughing: "Dan, they don't know what's goin' on!"

Mr. Dude talked on and on. When he paused I would prompt him, and he'd continue talking.

His niece, so full of New Orleans hospitality, demanded that we stop the recording and have supper. After the feast was over, she said, "I told you Uncle was a talking machine!"

Mr. Dude said, "You can call me what you wanna, but the public need to know 'bout the good ol' days." We returned to the parlor and Mr. Dude spoke from three in the afternoon until nine at night. A half dozen times he paused to ask: "Should I mention some historical facts?"

I'd say, "Sure!"

* * *

"At the cease of fighting in the Civil War with guns, there was the period of reconstruction that has never stopped until this day. The South and New Orleans, humiliated by the Union army, Yankee invaders, carpetbaggers and scalawags, retaliated with all sorts of jimcrow, discriminating laws and restrictions against the Negro." Mr. Bottley had begun his story.

"One was that Negroes were prohibited from congregating in any public park under the penalty of fine and imprisonment. So that was the end of Congo Square, and the Sunday evening festivities moved to an open-air area uptown. Each Sunday the crowds became larger as the news spread. A well-to-do drayman, Mr. Andre Poree, whose mules and wagons hauled garbage for the city, stabled his teams on part of this open area. Mr. Poree, being a good businessman, saw how well the vendors were doing at selling food and refreshments, so he built a hall, a barn-like structure and an open-air pavilion. He fenced off the area and started giving dances, outings, spectator baseball games, greased pig chases, balloon launchings, and all sorts of public affairs. He called his establishment Lincoln Park, in honor of Abraham Lincoln. He had a big grand opening on Lincoln's birthday.

"He organized a baseball team, bought them uniforms and called his team the Lincoln Giants. His team would play other teams each Saturday and Sunday. The games would start at two in the afternoon and be over by four or four-thirty, no later then five p.m. When the game was over, a lot of people would leave, but there'd still be a thousand to two thousand people waiting for the festivities to start.

6

"The first attraction would be the catching of the greasy pig. That was one of the funniest sights I ever saw. Everybody would be waiting around for my brother Buddy to start the greasy pig contest. My brother would go to the slaughterhouse on a Saturday and buy a male pig which generally weighed about twenty pounds. He would pay about three dollars for the pig.

"On Sunday, about twelve o'clock, we would shave all the hair off this pig. I'd hold the pig and Buddy would shave it with a long handled razor. Then we would grease him with about a pound of lard and put him into a chicken crate until the contest was announced at about five in the afternoon. The crate was placed on the bandstand so that all could see him. All the youngsters would have their eyes on that pig all afternoon. They'd be arguing and boasting about how they were going to catch the pig.

"Just before the balloon went up, Buddy would get on the bandstand and announce the pig catching contest. This is how he announced it, his arms raised high, yelling out loud to the large crowd that gathered round him:

> " 'Ladies, gentlemen and friends. We are now about to start the thrilling and exciting wild pig catching contest. This is a contest that calls for great endurance, skill and courage. We have gone to great expense to purchase a genuine, authentic, thoroughbred Arkansas Razorback boarhog. He was captured in the wilds of the forest of the State of Arkansas. He is wild and vicious! This Razorback is no pet! He has never been touched by the hands of a human before captivity!'

"Buddy would look down at the youngsters crowded round the pig in a crate and yell: 'Stand back everybody! Give this wonderful beast some air!'

"The crowd would move back, and he'd yell:

> " 'We will now take this brave and fearless bundle of juicy pork chops out into the center of the Park and turn him loose and out of his cage of captivity! The contestant who has the courage, cunning, energy,

7

stamina and ability to catch this noble animal will
have, when the animal is slaughtered and dressed,
enough pork chops, chitterlings, trotters (that's his
feet!), hams and spare ribs to last the whole coming
winter season and the ears, tail, snout, skin and grunt
he can give to his poor relations!'

"Then the crowd would applaud. My brother would tell Buddy
Bolden to play a march. Bolden would get off the stand and start
blowing his horn. I would lift the crate to my shoulders and march
behind Bolden, followed by the large crowd. We would march all
around the Park, like a big parade. Everybody in the Park would be
in this parade. When we marched to the center of Lincoln Park, my
brother would raise his hand and count: 'One! Two! Three!' When
he hollered 'Three!' I'd open the crate, smack the pig real hard on
his behind, and he'd take off, running like a rabbit, with the crowd
behind him. That was exciting to see. It usually took at least five
minutes to catch the pig.

"The opening of Lincoln Park was a sellout and through its
existence it was New Orleans' most noted amusement center. As
time went by, there came the big club and hall building era, private
clubs and benevolent association halls. Public dances were given
on weekends, Fridays, Saturdays, Sunday afternoons and nights.
Mr. Poree used brass bands in the hall and string bands on the
outdoor pavilion. In the summer, on Sunday afternoons after the
ball games, people stayed and spent the evening enjoying the
music and the other attractions.

"Around 1890 the star attractions were Buddy Bolden and
Buddy Bottley:

MR. ANDRE POREE
PRESENTS
– THE TWO BUDDIES –
• BUDDY BOTTLEY AND BUDDY BOLDEN'S BAND •

In the hall where the twelve or fourteen piece brass band played,
the elderly folks sat, listening or dancing to the sedate schott-
isches, quadrilles, lancers, waltzes, one-steps and an occasional
blues. In those days no one would think of dancing to a hymn or a
spiritual like *The Saints* or *Down by the Riverside*. Buddy Bottley

8

was all over the place. He was master of ceremonies, made all announcements and directed all activities: dashing out of the hall onto the pavilion, dancing in front of the band and singing and clapping his hands.

"There were dozens of small string groups and bands and at that time among the most popular were Mr. Charlie Sweet Lovin' Galloway, Punkie Valentin, Señor Butts and Pinchback Touro. Buddy Bolden was the most popular of all, but he was jealous of the great rhythms, showmanship and popularity of Mr. Sweet Lovin' Galloway with his fiddle and mandolin solos, especially since Galloway was a clown and had an engaging personality and a large following. He featured three terrific horn blowers who loved to battle Bolden's band. They were Edward Clem, cornet; Frankie Dusen, trombone; and Frankie Lewis, clarinet. Bolden started scheming and figuring how to break up that band, so he fired Brock Mumford, his guitarist, and clarinetist Willie Warner as well as trombonist Willie Cornish. Then, he connived and hired Galloway's men: he hired Frankie Dusen, Frankie Lewis and the banjoist Lorenzo Staulz. When Bolden stole Galloway's key men, he took all the steam and fire out of Sweet Lovin' Galloway's band. Galloway just faded from the picture when these men left.

"Dusen and Lorenzo Staulz sang, and with Buddy's foul songs and talk, that trio had the reputation of being the nastiest talking men in the history of New Orleans, and that also includes the Red Light District. When they arrived on the bandstand they greeted each other with such nasty talk as, 'Is your mother still in the District catchin' tricks?' 'They say your sister had a baby for a dog.' 'Don't worry about the rent, I saw your mother under the shack with the landlord.' These three men could go on insulting you for hours if you played 'the dozens.'

"Lorenzo Staulz was a past master at the game of playing the 'dirty dozens.' Back of the stand at Lincoln Park there was a large room, and all the underworld loved Lorenzo because he was always jolly, constantly joking and saying things funny, telling jokes on himself and describing all the latest scandals in a very funny way. The pimps, hustlers, gamblers and notorious bad men

9

would congregate up in that room and bring drinks for Lorenzo and the band. When the band would take a recess, no sooner would Lorenzo step into the room than they would point out one of the notorious characters and say to Lorenzo, 'Renza, this rat bastard was talkin' 'bout your dear old mother in a nasty way.'

"Then Lorenzo would blink his eyes and take a drink and look at the fellow and say, 'What did he say 'bout my mother?'

" 'He said your mother is a two cent whore.'

"Then Lorenzo would start: 'Since the subject is mothers, I'll tell you 'bout his mother, his mother's mother and her mother. They was the lowest bunch of low-lifed bitches that ever walked the face of the good Lord's earth.'

"Then the crowd would roar with laughter. And he'd continue: 'His family is so low down, ain't none of them ever been in or seen the insides of a church. He was born out of wedlock. Instead of his father raping his mother, his mother raped his father. Two days before he was born his grandfather took his simple-assed father and his no good mother to the preacher. Instead of a shotgun he had a Civil War cannon. When the preacher looked and saw these three notorious sons of bitches at the church door he almost fainted from shock. He said, "Oh no! You all cain't come in this church!" He led them way out behind the church where nobody couldn't see 'em, way out in the back yard next to the outhouse and performed the ceremonies there. He didn't even open the Bible. After he finished the marriage he told them to stay back there until night time when it's pitch dark and then sneak out one by one, and he made them swear that they wouldn't tell nobody he married them.'

"When Lorenzo would finish one of these classic dozens, the room would be in an uproar of laughter. Then he would say very nicely: 'I didn't say all that, fellows. Mr. Bolden said all that.' Lorenzo Staulz should have been a comedian. He could tell a million jokes and rhyme up anything. If you gave him a name he would start rhyming. He could rhyme it decent or uncouth.

"The combination brass and concert bands that played at Lincoln Park were Peerless, Cousto, Desdune, Jim Humphrey, Onward and Excelsior.

10

"This old guard was a very smart group, and with the advent of so many benevolent societies and social clubs being organized, they formed bands which would fit the budget of any organization that hired them. Most of the large organizations engaged large brass bands to sit and play at their affairs. (Fairgrounds, Lincoln Park, etc.) These bands used twelve men or more. Then smaller groups began to appear at these affairs, groups of seven or eight men.

"The seven instruments would sound good: violin, cornet, trombone, clarinet, bass fiddle, guitar and drums. Here were the big voices of the brass band: cornet, trombone and clarinet, backed up and supported by the string sounds that had been popular in Europe since the days of old masters like Paganini. There were dozens of competent violinists. Quite a few men of color had studied in France. The Creole societies which were very *ultra* had, for many years, supported a very fine classical orchestra. The violinist played an important part in the first jazz bands. First – he added dignity; second – he played the lead; most times he was also the instructor as musical knowledge and technique was not too fine in many of these bands. Musicians were highly respected when they could cut the mustard; that is, sight read.

"There was keen rivalry and much competition amongst these violinists and all other instrumentalists. Remember, press agents and magazine spreads were unheard of in those days. You had to outblow, outplay, your competitors, like Jelly Roll said, because you had your fans and loyal followers who boasted of your greatness. Since each section of the city had its idol you had to be sharp in contests or lose your prestige and with it future jobs and engagements, for the news would spread like wildfire when a Czar was toppled off his throne and many of the old boys took to their cups after a skirmish. The cats in the corner bar-rooms and barrelhouses (rough characters like Dirty Dog, Steel Arm Johnny and Butterfoot) were multi-murderers and chain gang graduates who, with very uncouth descriptions, would humiliate an ex-star and drive him to tears and more alcohol. Wherever he went the ovation was absent and instead he was greeted with contemptible facial expressions. It was a terrible thing, as Jelly Roll Morton

11

would say, 'when the feathers had been plucked from the peacock's tail.'

"There were jazz bands of six, seven and eight pieces, but the string groups were the most popular because they were more rhythmic and spirited with the violin, guitar and mandolin, and a few also added the accordion and the concertina.

"The younger crowd at Lincoln Park preferred the pavilion and the raggy rhythms of the smaller bands. But now concerning refreshments at affairs, in the old days, beer was the big seller. Next came punch and then lemonade. Fruits were also sold: oranges, apples, pears, peaches, and mandarins. When a young lady attended a dance she wore a head kerchief which served two purposes. One, as protection from the damp night air. Also the kerchief was used to carry home the fruit, for the custom was that a young man would take a young lady to the fruit bar and buy her a fruit of her choice before he danced with her. This fruit she gave to her chaperone to hold during the course of the evening. And there was always that solemn-faced old chaperone: a mother, an old aunt, or some ancient relative or neighbor. If the girl was pretty and jolly she took home dozens of fruits."

* * *

As Mr. Bottley continued to relate his boyhood memories of Lincoln Park, the Frenchman and his balloon and the two Buddies, he soon forgot his attempts at careful and proper diction. He lit his pipe, leaned back in his chair and talked on and on until he finally relaxed. A smile lit up his face as he spoke to me of his women, his eyes were bright when he talked, for he was back in his youth, reliving those scenes. He went on:

"On Sunday evenings at Lincoln Park, the main attraction was Buddy Bottley and the balloon. At five o'clock in the afternoon the brass band set up on the pavilion and played a long fanfare and lots of military march introductions.

"A Frenchman on a wagon, which was drawn by two horses would enter the park, and it was then announced that the dare-devil, the brave Mr. Buddy Bottley, would sail up in the air

12

in his balloon. The large crowd inside the park would gather around the balloon, while the second line on the outside waited anxiously for it to ascend.

"While the Frenchman and his assistants rigged up the balloon, the brass band struck up:

" 'You got wings,
I got wings,
All God's chilluns got wings.
I'm gonna fly all over God's heaven, heaven, heaven,
When I get to heaven
I'm gonna fly all over God's heaven.'

"The band played the spiritual until the balloon had ascended and disappeared out of sight, followed by the Frenchman on his wagon and the large second line. When the balloon eventually descended to the ground, the Frenchman and his assistants would retrieve it out of a tree, or from the top of a house, or electric wires.

"When I was a very small boy, in the evening, around dusk, you would look up and see a balloon sailing overhead. Or you'd hear someone yelling, 'Oh! Look at the balloon!' Balloon sailing was a very popular sport around the beginning of the century. The French brothers Piccard were very famous balloonists and set many world records, so naturally New Orleans went for the excitement of the sport. There were toy balloons that the stores sold, in a variety of sizes from three feet up. These were made of silk paper and very pretty. The paper was pasted together in a variety of brilliant colors and at the base was a round wire or wooden hoop. The wire was criss-crossed onto the hoop and a ball of rag or cotton was attached to the center. Gasoline was poured on the rag and while some tall boys or men held the balloon open in an upright position, a match was put to the gasoline soaked ball. As the smoke filled the balloon it would expand and become lighter than air and start to rise skyward as the crowd of kids followed it, running until it was out of sight.

"Everyone enjoyed the sport, but it was a fire hazard because the balloon sailed on and on until the fireball burnt out, then it descended, and where it came down there was more excitement because there was another gang of men and boys running after it to retrieve it. The sport came to a close when a large balloon landed on the poorhouse and set it afire. It was a sad sight to see all those old people trying to escape the flames: they were in wheelchairs, on crutches, crawling and praying for help. So the fire and police officials made it a felony to sail a model balloon.

"Going up in real balloons was very popular in those days and there were quite a few people in the balloon business. All the parks featured the sport: City Park, Audubon Park, the Fairgrounds, Jefferson Park and the two Negro parks: Lincoln and Johnson Parks. The balloons the white people went up in had baskets on them. A driver went up with two or more people, and it cost five dollars a passenger.

"This Frenchman at Lincoln Park had a small, sorta homemade balloon, which wasn't as big as these other balloons. The Lincoln Park balloon was sent up in a dangerous sorta way and you had to be brave to ride it and know how to maneuver this thing.

"The balloon was made of some kinda silk material, like what they use for raincoats. It was about twelve feet wide and about twenty feet tall. At the bottom was a nozzle like an elephant's snoot that was 'bout three feet round and six feet long. Around the middle of the balloon about two feet apart hung ropes which men would hold until the balloon stood in a position to start rising. Now whoever was going up had to be brave because there was no basket on this balloon, only a seat like a swing in a playground. Before you got on the swing seat the Frenchman put a harness round your waist and backsides like on a parachute and strapped you to the seat.

"The seat the rider sat on was connected to lots of ropes that hung from round the middle of the balloon. When it was sailing, you went dangling about ten feet under it. There was a long rope you had to hold in your right hand, so when you wanted to come back to earth you could pull it. Each time you pulled it you let some of the smoke out of the balloon, so if you felt you had had enough fresh air you could come down.

"Now, to get the thing full of smoke, the Frenchman had a contraption like an oven that the nozzle fit over like a glove. His assistants held the balloon upright with long poles they hooked in rings round the middle. In the side of this oven they made a fire and threw on gasoline tar, old sacks and a bit of water to make a strong black smoke. This black smoke went up the oven chimney, through the nozzle and into the balloon. When the balloon filled up, the Frenchman and his assistants had to hold the ropes tightly because the balloon started raring and moving; restless, just like a wild horse.

"The men held the ropes until the Frenchman tied a string around the nozzle. Then he'd holler, 'Let her go!' Everybody would turn the ropes loose, and whoever was riding started running with the balloon until it lifted them off the ground. Then the crowd would scream, and the second line on the outside would follow the balloon, running and yelling 'til it comes down. The Frenchman gets his wagon and races his team after it.

"Buddy Bottley was the first at Lincoln Park to sail. That's one reason why he was so popular. He knew how to maneuver that thing perfect. Each time he went up he went higher, and the Frenchman would raise hell, because you had to have enough smoke in the balloon or you would crash down to the ground, and he would have to follow for too far a distance.

"Bottley went up one time too often. This time somebody held the rope too long when the Frenchman yelled 'Let her go!' The balloon started rising sideways and threw Bottley off his feet. It dragged him along and pitched him upside the hall before dragging him off over the roofs of houses. He had the presence of mind to pull the rope and to hold it 'til enough smoke was let out so the balloon couldn't rise. When the second line got to him and held the balloon he was in bad shape and bloody as a hog. It was a pitiful sight to see all that black smoke and Bottley all banged up. The Frenchman laid him in the wagon and rushed him to the Charity Hospital. He stayed there about three weeks and came out walking on crutches.

"After the balloon accident, Bottley was never the same.

15

He still managed Lincoln Park, but was all crippled. When you saw him he either had a crutch or a walking cane. So his popularity faded away and the women stopped chasing him. Things went on as usual and now and then Bottley would get up and perform, if he felt in the mood, because occasionally the crowd would call, whistle, scream and clap their hands until he done something. The Frenchman would be there every Sunday with his team and the balloon, because Mr. Poree hired the balloon to advertise and publicize Lincoln Park. Once it went up and the second line started running, the commotion was sure to draw a crowd. Nobody would go up, and so they started offering five dollars, ten dollars, thirty dollars, but nobody took a chance.

"Then Reverend Sunshine Money, who was a famous preacher, gave a big revival meeting for one week and being 'notoriety', announced that he was going to sail the balloon up to heaven and bless and pray for all the sinners in New Orleans.

"The church people packed and jammed the park. The Frenchman was very happy, and he and Bottley gave Rev. Sunshine the instructions carefully. The Sunday he went up, the park was full of other preachers, ministers, deacons, elders, bishops, mothers, daughters and sisters who came up and shook Rev. Sunshine's hand and wished him luck and Godspeed on his soul-saving journey. Rev. Sunshine followed instructions and sailed up fine. But he went up too high. He became frantic, pulled the rope and let the smoke out too fast, which caused the balloon to swish quickly to the ground.

"When the Frenchman arrived on the scene to get his balloon, the Reverend had landed in a yard full of vicious bull-dogs. With tears in his eyes, the Frenchman put the chewed up balloon and the ragged Reverend into the wagon, and rushed Rev. Sunshine home so he could change his messed up underwear and put on another clean suit. From then on, the people of New Orleans sang a song that became very popular:

" 'The balloon started swingin', voop-to-voop,
Rev'an Sunshine Money went poop-to-poop'

"Reverend Sunshine was a great orator and a learned Biblical scholar. He could move his congregation to tears or a great feeling of spiritual happiness. A master showman, one of his main sermons was concerning dice, the lots that were cast for the Lord's garments. He used to boast proudly to the other preachers that his church belonged to him and not to his congregation, and that the deeds were vested in his name, so no deacons or elders would ever get ambitious and put him out of his church.

"Reverend Sunshine was always involved in some kind of scandal. I remember one time a sister in his church tooken very sick, and was at the point of death. The doctors told the family that it was just a matter of hours before she would pass away. Well, she being a very staunch member of Rev. Sunshine's church, he came to her bedside, prayed for her and consoled the family. When he noticed she was having the death rattles, he said to her: 'The Spirit of the Angel that is going to take our sick Christian soldier on her long, long journey is in our presence! Is in this domicile! So it is fitting and proper that I ask Sister So-and-so what is her last request before she departs from our midst and leaves to meet our maker.'

"The family became very still and serious as he leaned over and asked the sister: 'Sister So-and-so, what is it we could do and what would you want, that is within your poor family's means before you leave us?'

"The sister beckoned him to come closer as she weakly said, 'Rev'an Sunshine. I would like for John, my dear husband, to send all my kinfolks out in the yard and then come in here and get in bed with me for the last time. Please arrange that for me.'

"Reverend Sunshine called everybody in the kitchen, that is the older folks, and after heated argument, the husband John was sent into the bedroom to perform his wife's last request. The news spread all over town, and most of the folks I heared discussing a situation of that sort spoke up that since it was the wife's last earthly request and it should not be denied her, then that was the proper procedure for Reverend Sunshine to take.

"He always closed his sermon by blessing the white folks. After the ushers had passed the baskets for the third time, he'd bow his head, stretch forth his hands and direct his congregation to soften down the whispers, comments and outbursts, then he'd say, loud and sincerely, 'Sometimes I get the notion not to say what I am goin' to say, but the good and gracious spirit that guides me forces me to ask blessings for the people that continue to abuse my people. But I'm glad and very happy that the high officials in this great city of ours keep the criminal element in line in both races. So let's everybody here bow our heads while I ask blessings from above for our honorable and eminent city officials. First, let there be blessings for our dear Mayor and his family. Second, give the Chief of Police a searching eye to catch them criminals. Third, give all the judges in the Courthouse good health and keen judgement. And fourth, put an arm of protection around the police who patrol this wicked and sinful city! Amen!'

"There was a bunch of youngsters like today's jitterbugs, who idolized Bolden and Bottley, and they followed Bolden everywhere he played. They were great dancers, I'd say fanatics, and Bottley used to stage contests between them. The best dancer was a cute little girl named Annie Jones. Bottley enticed her to sail the balloon, and up she went. There was a strong breeze that Sunday, and the balloon sailed on and on and out of sight. Everybody in the park was downhearted and sad. Everybody just stood around, nobody danced and Bolden played hymns and blues all evening. The Frenchman came back with the police and the police said little Annie must have gotten scared and fainted and that if she did fall in the Gulf of Mexico or the Mississippi River that they, the police, would locate her. With that, all her friends started screaming and crying and Lincoln Park was a sad sight to behold.

"A week passed, and no word was heard of Annie. The following Monday, Annie came to the Park. She said she forgot all about pulling the rope, and that she had landed in the swamps around thirty miles below New Orleans. Some Cajun trappers saw her when the balloon came down. They rescued her and she stayed at their camp, but they could not bring her in right away because they had just set their traps. So she waited 'til the skins were gathered and then they brought her to New Orleans.

"I never saw the Frenchman or the balloon again."

"Now getting back to the two Buddies. They were bosom buddies and their headquarters was at Buddy Bolden's barber shop. In the rear was Bolden's office and residence. The two Buddies were always immaculately dressed, superbly groomed and both wore expensive clothes. They dressed like the wealthy southern gentlemen; no box-back coats for them – they were fashion plates. Both Buddies were, as the saying goes, 'lady killers' and very amorous gents.

"The Buddies had a plentiful supply of the most beautiful young ladies in New Orleans. Beautiful women would come alone to Lincoln Park or any place where Bolden played and just stand there in front of the band, stand and just sigh and mope around him. If he called one of them she ran to the master just like a little female dog. His power over them women was a mystery to me and all the other young men who went to Lincoln Park.

"Many a night after the dance ended I'd stick around because the two Buddies would be surrounded by a gang of pretty women. Bottley would see me looking all downhearted and he'd say, 'Dude, take this girl home with you and spend the night with her. I've got a lot of business to straighten out.' Then sho 'nuff, the woman would come and spend the night with me and make me very happy. It's a funny thing, but when I'd see her at Lincoln Park again, she'd be standing in front of the band looking sad at Bolden and Bottley, and would ignore me completely. It was a bitter pill for me to swallow, as you can see how good I look at eighty-two years of age, and you can imagine how handsome I was at twenty years old. In fact everybody who knew I was Buddy Bottley's brother thought I was the better looking.

"There was a lot of women switching between them Buddies, they had some agreement whereby they would let one another sample each other's women and they seemed to get a lot of enjoyment out of it. Bottley would give some guy a woman and think nothing of it but Bolden was different – he never gave up no woman. He'd take two or three home with him. He sure could hypnotize a woman – he was like a god or something. He'd come to play with three or four women trailing behind him. One carrying his horn, one carrying his hat, another toting his alcohol

19

and all of them behaving like sisters. He had 'em trained. As soon as the music started, these women would go and sit by the side of the platform and be peaceful like little lambs: pretty girls, just like they was in the amen corner, and wouldn't say a mumbling word. They would just look at the other women moping over Bolden but they never cause no confriction. You see, Bolden, being a barber, he was always smelling sweet like them whores in the District, nice and sweet, and maybe he used to sprinkle himself with that Van-Van water to draw woman to him like those Creole whores from downtown used to use. Dan, another thing, he always talked soft and easy and did not ignore no woman no matter how ugly she was.

"One night I saw him dedicate a tune to a woman. She looked like a dressed-up bear and he kissed her in the mouth 'cause it was her birthday. When the crowd saw that, they was for him, more so 'cause he wasn't a prejudiced person. That put all them crowjanes, alleybats and strumpets right in his corner, and those were the majority of women who came to Lincoln Park.

"I used to love going to Lincoln Park on Monday nights because on Monday nights, all them pretty whores would come to the park all dressed up with their pimps and madames. That's when you should have heard Bolden blow that cornet. His music was like medicine, made you feel happy and made you feel great. He'd play them low, lowdown-under blues and them whores would perform something terrible 'til they'd get out of hand, shaking down to the floor and dropping their drawers and teddies: that was a beautiful sight to see.

"Around eleven o'clock the crowd would get heated up and Buddy would play such nice love songs – like:

If You Don't Like My Potatoes, Why Do You Dig So Deep
Your Mammy Don't Wear No Drawers, She Wears Six Bit Overalls
Stick it Where You Stuck It Last Night
Let me Be Your Li'l Dog Till Your Big Dog Comes
Don't Send Me No Roses 'Cause Shoes Is What I Need
Pretty Pretty Mama, Open Your Legs One More Time
All The Whores Like the Way I Ride

20

A Memory of King Bolden

Melpomene Street Blues
The Bucket's Got A Hole In It
Make Me A Pallet On Your Floor

"Some nights early, around seven o'clock, Mr. Poree would come to the back of the bandstand and talk to the band because Lincoln Park catered to two types of people: real high class, respectable, influential colored people who would be having an affair in the main dance hall, school teachers, doctors, lawyers, dentists, druggists, the cream of the city's upper crust. Mr. Poree would call Bolden, my brother Buddy, and the rest of the band together and plead with them to take it easy with the lowdown music and the filthy songs. Then he would go back over to the dicty dance and associate with all the aristocrats because he was a high-class man. The band would all agree to 'keep it clean', then when he had left Bolden would snicker and say 'He's full of crap. Just for that I'm gonna turn it on tonight.' Lorenzo would laugh and say 'I'll sing hymns.'

"Bolden could play real nice and sweet, real pretty, nice and soft, especially on Sundays when he played the five o'clock matinees. Then Renza would sing the popular songs. But around nine o'clock when the low-life characters came out of the District, the notorious pimps, gamblers, hustlers, they would listen awhile to Bolden's sweet music. They would soon bring up money and raise particular hell about the music: 'Bolden, what's wrong with you, playing that sweet crap?'

"Bolden knew how to control a crowd perfect with that horn of his. You couldn't get near the platform 'cause the crowd would be so congested. Lots of folks would faint and pass out from the heat and the strong body odor, 'cause there wasn't many colored people who had bath tubs in those days. In fact, very few white folks owned one. Lots of times when the crowd would be jammed in front of Bolden he would stop blowing, take his hat and fan the air in front of him and holler loud:

'MY CHILLUN'S HERE. I KNOW IT 'CAUSE I CAN SMELL 'EM.'

"That used to tickle the crowd, and everybody would clap, scream,

21

laugh and holler. I'm tellin' you when that odor used to rise it smelled like burnt onions and train smoke, and I'd think of it whenever I'd hear Buddy Bolden holler 'bout smelling his children.

"If I wasn't dancing with some gal I would push my way through the crowd and get up on the platform. Me being always around my brother and Bolden, the crowd would let me push through. Bolden would blow the blues so sad, then exciting, and he had that handkerchief to wipe his mouth and it looked like he was thinking far, far, far away. He never got tired and when it was hot, he always kept his coat on 'cause he wore them expensive alpaca and mohair suits like rich white folks. The other music men took off their coats, but not Bolden.

"Frankie Dusen and the banjo player, Lorenzo Staulz, were also very popular with the women, as well as being, as I said, the most nasty and foul talking men I think that ever walked the face of the earth. I had thought that Willie Cornish talked and sang nasty, but when them two joined Bolden's band the things they said and sang made Cornish sound like a church deacon! Now, Lorenzo had a nice singing voice and could sing nice if he wanted to, but the people just wanted him to sing nasty. He could rhyme up words fast as lightning to any song.

"He'd be singing a song nice and decent and sweet and the crowd would come close to hear him, as in those days there wasn't no microphone. When the crowd would get packed real close up in front of the band, Bolden would growl and grunt real loud, 'Sing the song, Renza,' and Dusen would say, 'Put 'em in the alley, Mr. Lorenzo Staulz,' and Lorenzo would start singing real lowdown and nasty. The way he would sing that nasty talk would make the skin on your flesh twitter. Many of the women would hold their ears and rush away from the band. Even them lowdown whores would walk off and pull their men away. Lorenzo sang the *Salty Dog* song real funny and the crowd would scream at the words:

> 'I got a woman who's big and fat
> She would come and git me but she don't know where I'm at
> Doing the ballin' the jack; doing the ballin' the jack
> I'm so glad she's big and fat
> She's got crabs on her belly, doing the ballin' jack.'

"Dusen and Bolden used to get a great big happy feeling when Lorenzo sang. He could sing *Funky Butt* for an hour; he could sing all day and all night if he wanted to, because he would sing about all the notoriety whores, pimps, madames and even about the policeman at the door. Of course the policeman did not ever hear all the nasty lowdown things Lorenzo would be singing about him and the police department, the mayor, the governor, the president. He would even sing about the Civil War; about how General Grant made Jeff Davis kiss and kiss his behind and how General Sherman burnt up Georgia riding on Robert E. Lee's back. The crowd would scream and holler but Lorenzo would stand up and sing about them white folks with his eyes watching the policeman on the door. The policeman would not know what he would be singing but Lorenzo was protecting his head and taking no chances. One chorus I'll always remember was:

> 'I thought I heer'd Abe Lincoln shout,
> "Rebels, close down them plantations and let all them niggers out."
> I'm positively sure I heer'd Mr. Lincoln shout.
> I thought I heard Mr. Lincoln say,
> "Rebels, close down them plantations and let all them niggers out,
> You gonna lose this war; git on your knees and pray
> You gonna lose this war; git on your knees and pray!"
> That's the words I heer'd Mr. Lincoln say.'

"One night the crowd was laughing and hollering so loud that the policeman left the door and slowly started walking toward the bandstand. Lorenzo saw him coming and started making believe that he was coughing and choking. Bolden saw the police pushing through the crowd and he started blowing louder on his horn than I ever heard him blow before, and the crowd was wise and everybody started to dance. That was a very funny scene. Lorenzo had lots of pretty women and was always well dressed. He had a pressing and cleaning business. If you took your clothes to his place to have them cleaned, if he looked nice in your suit and it fitted him, he wore it. So, people naturally thought he had a hundred suits, but he was wearing other folks' clothes.

"Frankie Dusen had a few women; he was a tall handsome man, who looked like an Indian with a full head of black, straight, silky hair. Women went for him, but he loved to gamble. Many times Bolden would ask Dusen to come with him to the barber shop 'cause some fine pretty woman wanted to meet him, but Dusen would say, 'I'm going to a helluva cotch game this morning at Mustache's tonk.'

"Lorenzo Staulz would kid Bolden about his barber shop. When the dance was almost over, Bolden would have all these fine built, pretty women standing about waiting for the band to finish so they could go home with Mr. Bolden. When Mr. Bolden finished playing the last tune he would say, 'Who's going with me to the barber shop?'

"There would be a pause, because Dusen was going his way, Jimmy Johnson was going his way (and everyone in Bolden's band called Jimmy 'Old Folks' 'cause he would always pack his bass and sneak off and disappear somewheres out in the darkness.)

"Lorenzo Staulz, Renza, as they called him, would say: 'Bolden, we will now go to the butcher shop.'

"Bolden would laugh 'cause Lorenzo would kid Bolden, saying that Bolden did not have a barber shop – he had a butcher shop, because a man was risking his life if just once he sat in one of Bolden's three barber chairs. Renza would say, 'Bolden uses dead men's razors.'

Now, this is an insult to a barber, because it was customary, when a barber was called to shave a dead man, and did so, for that razor never to be used again. The razor was supposed to be hit with a hammer and destroyed or thrown in the garbage can, no matter how fine the razor was. That is why the barber's expensive charge was five dollars to shave a dead man. A first class razor, made of German steel, cost three dollars, so the barber charged five dollars and his profit was two dollars. All the price signs in barber shops if you looked at the bottom, would say: 'Dead Man Shave $5.00.'

"Some shops don't have that because many supposedly first class barbers are scared to shave dead people. I know one barber went to shave a dead man who was in the undertaking parlor lying dead on the cooling board. While the barber shaved the stone cold dead man, some gas escaped out of the deceased and made a long, deep, bass sound. The barber heard the sound and dropped dead from fright. So there was two funerals, and that is the only time I know of a stone cold, dead man killing a living man.

"When the ambulance came and examined the dead barber and pronounced him dead, the barber's wife got suspicious and figured there was something funny about her husband's death. She got herself a lawyer to handle the case. So the white folks figured they could make some money and started a investigation. Detectives, the District Attorney, the prosecuting attorney, the coroner, civil sheriff and all the law authorities went behind closed doors. Then they came to the verdict the barber had a weak heart.

"Many times when a poor man dies his wife has no money to have him embalmed, so he has to be buried quickly. So he's in the Geddes and Moss undertaking parlor on the cooling board, and his wife dickers with Mr. Moss and explains she has no money to give her man a big time funeral. The undertaker tells her to just have her dead husband shaved and bury him quick before he starts to smelling. Then she contacts her husband's barber who comes to the funeral parlor and shaves her husband. But, you see, when a dead man is on the cooling board for more than eight hours he gets full of gas and this dead poison gas has to come out of the deceased man's stomach, from his mouth or his rectum. A brave and experienced barber knows about gas and does not get excited when it is released.

"Lorenzo would say that all of Bolden's razors were dead men's razors. Lorenzo would say real loud when him and Bolden was getting all them fine women together to go to the shop, 'We are now going to King Bolden's butcher shop and cut some meat!'

"When I would hear that I would ask my brother Buddy, 'Can I come with you all?'

"Naturally he would say, 'Come on, Dude.'

"Then I would get in the procession and walk to the barber

shop 'cause I would get me one of them fine young fine-built pretty girls. All my brother Buddy would have to say is, 'Li'l girl, go on with my li'l brother.' And that was all. They would come on with me like a li'l lamb. Of course I would get the leavings, the crumbs off the table. But I would be satisfied and contented.

"Bolden always closed his dance with

'I thought I heer'd Mr. Bolden say,
"Funky butt, funky butt,
Take it away." '

"That tune would last about forty minutes and if you had your woman with you, you and her was supposed to do that last dance. It was a mad scramble to find the one who belonged to you. There were very few fights at Lincoln Park when Bolden played because he knew all the roughnecks and hoodlums and Mr. Poree had influence with the police, so most of the fights started a few blocks from Lincoln Park.

"Bolden and Bottley was good to all the criminals who were down and out and saw that many of them had a square meal and lodgings. So if either of them said, 'Break up the humbug,' it was broken up promptly. Sometimes Bottley would leave Lincoln Park with a sack of women and behind them would be these rats, following along like scavengers. If he walked to his place or Bolden's barber shop, when he reached the door he would give all them rats a pretty woman who would not speak to them the next time they met in public.

"Bottley had a lot to answer for 'cause he gave a lot of simple girls to them pimps and hustlers in the District. That's a fact. But not Bolden, 'cause he kept them for hisself.

"Bottley's favorite saying when he looked at a crowd of women, he'd rub his hands in one another, smile and say, 'Look at our women: just like a rainbow. All colors, just like a bouquet of roses.'

"Them Monday nights at Lincoln Park was something to see. When them madames and pimps brought their stables of women to hear Bolden play, each madame had different color girls in her stables. For instance, Ann Jackson featured mulatto girls; Maud Wilson featured high browns and so forth and so on. And them different stables was different colors just like a bouquet.

"In them days, there was a lot of dope around, and it was common to the people in the underworld. You could get any kind of narcotic you wanted if you could pay the price. Morphine, cocaine, opium, hasheesh and Mexican cigarettes. There was a man named Sweet Candy who could get you any kind of dope you wanted 'cause the law was not strict like it is today. So when the underworld wanted somebody they tricked you on the habit. They would make sweet lovin' to you and then, when you were off your guard, they would coax you to try some nose candy, and if you was simple you naturally would sniff the harmless looking white powder. And once you started you were a junkie, hooked with a very bad, an expensive, habit.

"Those District people love to put a fool in the same boat with them because misery loves company. The pimps used to trick poor little pretty Cajun gals, from out the country and off them plantations, and them cold-blooded whores used to get them foolish boys and simple men thataway. They called cocaine 'nose candy,' and a lot of simple people think it is candy, sure enough, until they get the habit. Then, whoever tricks you can make you do anything they want you to, because they are your master. When you get the crave and the sweats and the possum dancing on your back, you are in pitiful shape.

"Them pimps and whores loved to see a young fool humbalizing and craving for dope, because they was tricked and had gone through the same predicament. The two Buddies was the favorite of all them District and underworld people, and lots of times I would go with them to the wild parties those District madames would give – and I'm telling you they were wild.

"Now, Bolden's barber shop was small but very neat and clean. His customers were mostly sporting people who spent their money freely. Bolden did not cut just anybody's hair, he picked his customers: in other words, he had to know you personally. If not, one of his other two barbers called out, 'Who's next?'. When you sat in Bolden's chair you were expected to get the whole works, haircut, shave, massage and shampoo and then, when he finished with you, you had a new head and you smelled just like those District women. Lots of men let Bolden work on them just to be big shots.

"When Bolden wasn't busy cutting hair, he would sit or stand on the outside and talk and joke with all the children in the neighborhood; he was famous and he was their idol. When business was slow on other days, he would be in the rear of his shop where there were three rooms he lived in, and he would blow his horn for some of them pretty women, pimps, and gamblers. There was always some women in the barber shop going in his house, and that is why it was so popular. Yes, Bolden was idolized by everybody; even the dicty people who did not like his music had respect for him. The children really loved him. He would buy them candy and if he felt good he would take as many as a dozen small boys inside the barber shop and quickly give all of them 'all-offs': that is, clip all the hair off their heads. Nothing fancy or careful; just clip all the hair off. That used to tickle him because some of the mothers would get mad when they saw their boys' shiny bald heads.

"Buddy got more popular and more popular. He was the king. Yes, he was the king and all the other musicians came to wherever he played to hear him and to copy his style.

"But Bolden went to the dogs too. He went crazy as a bedbug. There was a gang of stories about what happened to him. Some folks said one of his women hoodood him with human dust. I knew the woman, but I can't think of her name now. She was a brownskin woman, the serious kind. She wasn't his wife, but like his main woman. She was the only one who had keys to his place. She did his laundry, cleaned the house, sometimes cooked for him and I guess lotsa times came to his place and saw him laying up with other women. They may not say nothing, but women don't like that.

"They say she went to a hoodoo woman and got some human dust and put it in his food to make him love her. The rumors was that she wanted Bolden to settle down, save his money and marry her. But Bolden put her down. She managed to get friendly with him again and pulled that trick. These voodoo people go in the graveyards and get deadfolks' bones, burn them to dust and fix you. Bolden started acting funny. He stopped wearing them whitefolks' clothes and started wearing box-back suits and colored folks' clothes. There was a big change in his appearance and looks 'cause before he had worn those high class expensive white folks' clothes which the average poor colored man couldn't afford. That was not the colored style, and colored folks would laugh at you. But nobody laughed at Bolden and Bottley. They was big shots. They had class.

"One day Bolden and this woman got into an argument and started fighting. He beat her up terrible and she ran from the rear through the barber shop and into the street naked, in broad daylight. One of the barbers rushed out and covered her up with a barber cloth and the next-door neighbor let her in the house and hid her under the bed. Bolden sat on the neighbor's steps with two razors for the rest of the day and most of the night. The news spread and all of his friends arrived on the scene to try to calm him down which proved useless. But that neighbor never opened her door, which was a very sensible thing to do.

"After that rumble, the barbers would hear Bolden talking and arguing in the rear and when they went into the back he would be looking in his mirror and fussing with himself. When a woman would come to visit him, he would lock up the rear and keep the woman there for days, drinking whisky and threatening the woman with razors if she attempted to leave. So all his friends drifted away.

"Here is how the public and his friends found out he was crazy. One day a gambler, Tom Pickett, came to the shop to get his hair cut and the whole works. As was the usual conversation in Bolden's shop, Pickett and Bolden started joking about women. I knew this kidding between Pickett and Bolden was going to end up bad because they would get too personal. I noticed that Bolden would get nervous and his hands would start shaking when he was shaving somebody and Pickett would be talking about his women. Yet every time that Pickett sat in Bolden's chair this kidding about women would start. Buddy would not show anger, but I would see he did not like what Pickett would say. This par-

29

ticular evening I thought sure hell would break loose.

"Pickett told Bolden, 'Sweet man, how do you keep tabs on all your women? You can't watch all of them.'

"Bolden frowned and said, 'I don't have to watch no women, they watch me. That's what they pay their admission for; they pays to come to Lincoln Park and stand around the band stand to look at me, the King. To hear me play. It does them so much good just to see me. I can tell the look on their faces, and sometimes I try them out. I have perfect control over them. I can make them feel and put them in any mood I wants to. I can blow and make 'em feel blue. I can blow and make 'em feel sad. I can blow and make 'em feel glad. I can blow and make 'em feel the spirit. And I can make 'em start fighting. I just have to start blowing my baby and I can make that Lincoln crowd do anything.'

"Pickett said, 'Who's your baby?'

"Bolden growled, 'My baby is my horn that's who. The King can make 'em do anything he wants them to do – and that goes for the men too – you all knows that that's the natural fact. They come up to me and asks me to play certain tunes and by that I know they want me to make certain tunes and by that I know they want me to make them feel a certain way. And, Pickett, you know that many times you have come to the band stand with one of them big fat bears you like to dance with and ask me to play that tune, *Let Me Be Your Li'l Dog Till Your Big Dog Comes*. The reason you want that tune is that you are tryin' to trap that bear, make her think you love her. Ain't that right?'

"Pickett laughed and said: 'I ain't talkin'.'

"Bolden said, 'But you admit you go crazy about those big fat bears, don't you Pickett. Answer up, Pickett!'

"Pickett said, 'Bolden, do you truly believe that you can get any woman in this city that you wants?'

"Bolden says, 'Tell me you don't like bears.'

"Pickett says, 'If you will tell me honestly that you truly believe that you can have any woman in the city of New Orleans, I will admit that I am fond of bears.'

"Bolden says, 'I don't want to lie but so far, knocking on wood, I have never been turned down, not King Bolden.' And when he says 'Knocking on wood,' he raps Pickett's skull with the knuckles of his hand, kind of hard. You can tell Pickett don't like that. Bolden goes on, 'I do the turning down. Nightly I turn down dozens, hundreds. I hate to do it, but I got to get some rest. Does that set you right, Pickett?'

"Pickett rubs his head where Bolden had hit him. Sensing Bolden's anger he changes the subject. Pickett says nicely, 'What gave you the idea to write the song *Funky Butt, Take It Away*?'

"Bolden says, looking hard at the ceiling as he shaves Pickett just by the feel of his hand, 'Where I got the idea? It was no idea, it is a real fact. When I sing that song I mean what I am saying. When I'm playing inside a hall in the hot summer time and the big crowds of people are standing in front of me, the place gets stuffy and the funk starts to rising and flying. I sing "Open up them windows and let that foul air out!" and "Funky butt, take it away!" I mean that, I ain't jokin'. Sometimes I stop playin' until all them windows are wide open, every one of them.'

"When Bolden said those last words, Pickett relaxed in the chair like he was sleepin', and the conversation and kidding stopped. I was glad because Bolden was getting mad.

"Then suddenly Bolden shouted, 'I don't only sing *Funky Butt* at Lincoln Park. I sings it at any place I play, Tulane University or the river boats. Because white folks get awfully funky too. Any crowd of people, white, black, green, gray, will get funky when they start dancing close together and belly rubbing.'

"Bolden finished barbering Pickett. Pickett got out of the chair, paid Bolden, looked in the large mirror, felt his shaved head and rubbed the spot where Bolden had tapped him sharply. He put on his hat, said, 'So long, folks,' and walked out of the barber shop. He seemed angry to me.

"Bolden mumbled, 'That Pickett bastard. Always worryin' 'bout my women. He's jealous. I see him at Lincoln Park watching me and all my women with his mouth runnin' water like a timber wolf. There's just not a night that passes that he don't beg me to give him one of my women. Let him get his own! I'm gonna stop cuttin' his hair. I don't need his trade.' And Bolden walked to the back of the barber shop.

"One of the barbers said, 'I gets scared every time Pickett comes in here talkin' 'bout Bolden's women. Bolden don't like that. Someday there's gonna be trouble.'

"Two weeks later, my brother Buddy was in bed feeling bad. He was expecting some of his friends to come by. He asked me to go and fetch Bolden to give him a shave and a haircut. So I hurry over to the barber shop, and tell Bolden that Bottley is in bed sick and his broken bones are paining him. As I'm talking, Pickett struts in and sits in Bolden's chair. He says 'Hello King!'

"Bolden grumbles, 'Hello Pickett.'

"Pickett says, 'Give me the works.'

"Bolden puts the barber cloth round Pickett's shoulders and starts cutting his hair. He says to me, "Dude, as soon as I take care of Pickett, we go to see Buddy.'

"Pickett says, 'What's wrong with Buddy?'

"I say, 'He's sick. His arms, legs, back, all his bones are paining him.'

"Pickett laughs, saying, 'Yeah! All them women was too much for him. They finally caught up with him. He wanted every woman he saw.'

"Bolden says, 'That's a lie. The women wanted Buddy! The women ain't his trouble. He hurt himself flying that balloon.'

"Pickett says to Bolden, 'You're covering up for him. And by the way, sweet man, what you use to make all them women love you?'

"Bolden says, 'Kind treatment and special Bolden lovin'.'

"Pickett says, 'How many women you got now, sweet man?'

"Bolden says, 'So many I can't count. It's impossible to calculate the amount of women who loves me.'

"Pickett says, 'Name me all the pretty ones so I can git the ugly ones.'

"Bolden stopped cutting hair, frowned and then started calling names as he slowly started cutting Pickett's hair again: 'Clara, Mary, Annie, Bessie, Emma, Susie, Sarah, Nancy...' He went on and on calling names.

"When he finally stopped, all was quiet in the shop for a

32

few moments. Then Pickett said very softly, seriously and confidentially, 'Buddy, I hate to tell you, but you ain't got them women anymore.'

"And Buddy asked, surprised, 'Who took em?'

"Pickett says, 'I hate to tell you but they all belong to me; they are all my personal, private property.'

"The barber shop then became as quiet as a graveyard at midnight. Bolden continued to cut Pickett's hair, then went into the rear of the shop for about five minutes, while Pickett joked with the customers and other barbers about Bolden's silence. Bolden returned, pulled the lever on the barber chair which stretched Pickett out horizontal, in a shaving position. Buddy Bolden very slowly stropped his razor and prepared the mug of shaving lather. He shaved Pickett three times and he perfumed him sweetly and lathered his face again each time he shaved him. Each time he was shaved, Pickett would ask, 'Man, ain't you finished?'

"Bolden said, 'After this shave you won't need no more.'

"The people in the shop watched nervously. When Bolden went to the facebowl to make more lather Pickett jumped right out of the chair, burst open the doors and ran in the street, screaming, 'The man is crazy! The man is crazy!' At a safe distance he kept screaming and pointing at the barber shop. A large crowd gathered as Bolden stood in the door with a razor in his hand. The barbers and customers kept cool, which was a wise thing to do in a predicament like this. The news spread and everybody in the neighborhood came on the scene. The police came and Pickett told them what had happened, so they escorted him back to the shop. Bolden very calmly and peacefully informed the police that Pickett was the crazy one but the barbers slyly nodded to the police that Pickett had told the truth.

"The police took Bolden and Pickett to the police station and related the story to the captain. Pickett got down on his knees, kissed the Bible, and swore on the head of his dead mother and all his relatives and ancestors that he was not crazy and had told the honest truth.

"Bolden also got down on his knees and went through the

same act. The police captain sent them both to the Charity Hospital to be examined. The doctors decided that they were not crazy – but weak minded. In those days the doctors were not so scientific as they are today and to find out if a colored person was crazy they asked him five questions and judged him according to his answers:

"First – Do you like fried chicken?

"Second – Do you like watermelon?

"Third – Do you like gin and whisky?

"Fourth – Are you scared of ghosts and spirits?

"Fifth – When you die, will you see St. Peter at the Golden Gate with the golden keys and Gabriel blowing his horn?

"If you answered 'no' to any of those questions you was put in the crazy house till you came to your senses.

"Yes, the judge, lawyers, doctors would get their heads together in the judge's chamber whenever two ignorant people was involved with the law. Rather than take up all their time looking the research and record books of other crazy cases, they would just come to a quick conclusion and get rid of the case real quick. So they figgered chicken, gin, and watermelon were Southern delicacies that all sensible people liked.

"When the trial came up naturally the courthouse was crowded with friends of Bolden and Pickett. The judge asked Pickett if he worked. Pickett said, 'Judge, your honor, I don't have no steady job. I work here, there and most any place they need me.'

"The judge asked, 'What was your occupation and what kind of physical labor did you engage in to earn your livelihood and who was your last employer?'

"Pickett says, 'Judge your honor, the last man I worked for died five years ago and since that time I've been running games, that is, cotch and skin games.'

"The judge says, 'An occupation of that sort calls for a lot of sitting down, scheming and figuring and too much sitting down will make you get too fat and you will get muscle bound and rheumatism will set in your bones and you will give the people at Charity Hospital a lot of trouble. Is that right, Pickett?'

"Pickett bows his head and says, 'That is right, your honor.'

"The judge says, 'I am going to send you somewhere where you can get some exercise and that is the city workhouse.'

"Pickett had a police record and was sent to jail for sixty days, charged with vagrancy, no visible means of support, pandering and disturbing the public peace.

"Bolden, being well known and never in trouble before, was given a suspended sentence and forbidden to have a barber shop, cut hair or shave any citizen in the city of New Orleans. That put Buddy Bolden out of the barber business.

"Buddy Bolden's band had been the talk of the town for about twelve years. He always had more jobs than he could play, so many nights he'd go to two or three other halls just by himself and play a half dozen tunes with other bands. He'd put Edward Clem or Little Barrelhouse Bunkie Johnson on cornet in his main band to blow until he returned from playing with the other bands, and he'd come back and finish the night with his own band. While he'd be gone, Frankie Dusen would lead the band, call the tunes and be the leader. Then the trouble started. People would come to Buddy's barber shop and hire him, pay him a deposit, sign a contract for a certain date while Dusen would be somewhere else signing for jobs on the same dates. There would be arguments and confusion.

"The men took sides with Dusen because he was like the manager. Then Bolden and Dusen would argue because Bolden, working in the barber shop all day, would come to the job late, tired and sleepy, or send Little Black Bunkie, Clem or some other cornet man in his place. He just was killing himself, up all day, up all night, and so many women chasing and running him down. One time Bolden contracted three or four jobs and forgot to tell the band and that caused lotsa trouble and arguments. So the band called a meeting at the barber shop to try to get an understanding. Bolden said he really did not remember signing the contracts and admitted that sometimes he could not remember anything. So Bolden and the members of the band agreed that Dusen would be the manager and sign all contracts for jobs. Things ran smooth for about six months, then Bolden and his

35

main, number one woman got into that fight, and that was a big scandal in the neighborhood. On top of that, a week or two later, came the incident with Tom Pickett that caused Bolden to be in real trouble with the police authorities. Yes, after that scene with Pickett, Bolden began losing all his friends and followers. They figured he was crazy and knowing he was a barber reckoned he always had his razor on him. And his band got scared of him.

"After turning over the management of his band to Frankie Dusen, Buddy Bolden lost interest in it, because the other five members said very little to him. They followed his leadership and that's about all. The band learned no new songs; they just played the old favorites. They did not have no practise; everybody lost interest. The people stopped following the band and all them stray pretty women started to disappear. Dusen contracted an excursion and a picnic to Mobile, Alabama, on a Sunday. Buddy did not show up, so when the excursion got to Mobile, Dusen hired a Mobile cornet player.

"The next night, which was Monday, the band played at Lincoln Park and, after the dance, Dusen called a conference and told Bolden that he was fired. Bolden asked, 'What are you firing me for?'

"Dusen said, 'Because you did not show up yesterday at the excursion train.'

"Bolden said, 'Man, I plumb forgot all about that excursion.'

"Dusen said, 'You just forgot that you are in this band.'

"Bolden answered, real sad and pitiful, 'But this is my band.'

"Dusen said, 'It was your band, but it ain't no more.'

"It was a very sad scene. Bolden picked up his horn and walked out of Lincoln Park. When Frankie Dusen fired him out of his own band, that was the end of Bolden. He cried for days. There was lots or rumors that Bolden was going to kill Dusen, but nothing happened. So Dusen could not use Buddy Bolden's name in connection with the band any more. He changed the name to Frankie Dusen's Eagle Band, and he hired Little Barrelhouse Bunkie Johnson to play cornet in Bolden's place. Then that band

came to be real famous in the city. They would advertise themselves like this:

" 'The Eagle flies high and never loses a feather.
If you miss this dance you'll have the blues forever.'

* * *

"When Bolden slowly made his way out of Lincoln Park, not one
person said a word to him. Somebody went and told my brother
Buddy about Bolden and Dusen arguing, and that Dusen had fired
Bolden. My brother hurried to the bandstand as fast as his
crutches would take him there, for he was mad as General
Sherman when he was marching through Georgia. He limped up
to the bandstand and told Dusen, 'Stop the music!'

"Dusen did just that. Then they both went into the dressing
room which was next to the bandstand and started to argue. The
band went into the room and I followed. My brother said to
Dusen, 'Are you out of your mind firing the great Buddy Bolden?
Do you realize what you have done? Don't you know that Buddy
Bolden is the main star attraction here and without Bolden we'll
all be out of a job? Supposin' Bolden starts up another band and
starts playing at Johnson Park, don't you know the crowd will
follow him and close Lincoln Park?'

"Dusen said, 'Me and the band could not stand his foolish-
ment any longer. We have been putting up with him and his
bullshit for over three years.'

"My brother sees me standing there listening and says,
'Dude, go to Bolden's house and tell him if he's home to don't
leave, to wait there for me.' I left and went to Bolden's house.

"When I get there, the house is all dark, so I walk up the
steps and listen at the door. After about five minutes, I hear
something on the inside. I peep through the crack in the door. The
lamp is lit and I see that Bolden is sitting in a chair with his head in
his hands. His head is shaking – it looks like he is crying. Then I see
him take a handkerchief from his pocket and wipe his eyes. I felt so
sorry because the house was dark and dreary looking. None of his
friends were with him and now was the time he needed friends.

"I watch Bolden get up then he returns with a bottle in his left hand and his cornet in his right hand. He flops down in the chair, shakes his head and swallows a long drink from the whisky bottle. He starts coughing and drops the bottle on the floor. It looks like he is crying again. The tears came to my eyes too, and I got to thinking about how many thousands of people Bolden had made happy and all them women who used to idolize him and all of them supposed to be friends. 'Where are they now?' I say to myself.

"Then I hear Bolden's cornet. I look through the crack and there he is, relaxed back in the chair blowing that silver cornet softly, just above a whisper, and I see he's got his hat over the bell of the horn. I put my ear close to the keyhole. I thought I had heard Bolden play the blues before, and play the hymns at funerals, but what he is playing now is real strange and I listen carefully, because he's playing something that for a while sounds like the blues, then like a hymn. I cannot make out the tune, but after awhile I catch on. He is mixing up the blues with the hymns. He plays the blues real sad and the hymn sadder than the blues and then the blues sadder than the hymn. That is the first time in my recollection I had ever heard hymns and blues cooked up together. A strange cold feeling comes over me; I get sort of scared because I know the Lord don't like that mixing the Devil's music with his music.

"But I still listen, because the music sounds so strange and I am sort of hypnotized. I close my eyes, and when he blows the blues I picture Lincoln Park with all them sinners and whores, shaking and belly rubbing. Then, as he blows the hymn, I picture my mother's church on Sunday, and everybody, all the church folks, humming with the choir. The picture in my mind kept changing with the music as he blew. It sounded like a battle between the Good Lord and the Devil. Something tells me to listen and see who wins. If Bolden stops on the hymn, the Good Lord wins; if he stops on the blues, the Devil wins.

"As I am listening, a car turns the corner and pulls up in front of Bolden's shop. My brother hops out of the car on his crutches, followed by Dusen and Mr. Poree. He sees me and asks,

'Is Bolden in there?'

"I say, 'Yes, he is.'

" 'Are you sure?' he asks.

"I say, 'Yeah. He is in there, blowing the blues and the hymns, one after another, on his horn. He sounds so good I did not want to disturb him.'

"My brother says, 'Watch out!' And he hits the door with his crutch, real hard. I hear the music stop, but the crutch hit that door so loud and hard that I could not tell whose music Bolden stopped on, the Lord's or the Devil's. I was very disappointed.

"Bolden came to open the door and my brother said, 'It's me, Bottley.' And the four of us walked in. Bolden turned on the lamps in the barber shop, and my brother said, 'Bolden I'm sorry about what happened tonight. Before you left you should have spoken to me. We are the best of friends and always will be. Mr. Poree hired you and not Dusen. You have the agreement to lead the band at Lincoln Park. Your name is advertised and the patrons mainly come to hear you. Sure, I know you and Dusen have been arguing a long time, but I did not think it was real serious. I figured you all being two grown men understood each other's dispositions. Now I have spoken to Dusen and he came here to apologize to you for stepping over his bounds. He and the boys are sorry about the whole matter. Ain't that right, Dusen?'

"Dusen smiles, saying, 'Shake hands, Bolden. I want to apologize for talkin' too fast.'

"Bolden smiles as they firmly shake hands. My brother smiles. Mr. Poree smiles and I smile. They shake hands all around. Bolden goes to the rear of the shop and returns with a brand new bottle of whisky 'cause the bottle he dropped has spilled all over the floor. Bolden pulls the cork out and takes a long drink. Then he passes the bottle round and everybody drinks but Mr. Poree. He refuses, saying, 'Never touch the stuff.'

"Dusen then says, very sadly, 'Bolden, we have the most famous band in New Orleans, but we have nothing without you out there in the front line. Three men have to be in the front line or there is no front line. The people come expecting to see you blowing. When the band starts and you are not out there it is very embarrassing because the band don't sound right. For the last two years, the other five men don't know if you're going to play or not. They don't say nothing to you but they burn my ears off. We never know if you are going to play or not. It's nerve wracking. When you send Li'l Bunkie or Edward Clem or some other cornet player, seems like you send them at the last minute so they come a half hour or an hour late. Now that's been going on a long time. We played that excursion to Mobile, Alabama, and when the people didn't see you, they raised all kinds of hell. That's all uncalled for. When I ask you what happened, you shrug your shoulders and say you forgot. I even gave you a book with all the dance dates written down. Ain't that a fact, Bolden?'

"Bolden says, 'You are absolutely and perfectly right.' He then says, 'I am sorry Dusen. But as hard as I try I just cannot seem to remember nothing. Half of the time I don't know one day from another. Something's wrong with my mind. Last Sunday I opened up the barber shop thinking it was Monday. Something is wrong with me because barber shops don't open on Sunday.'

"Bolden laughed and we all joined in. Then Dusen said, 'It is still your band and always will be. Now let's get this confusion straight. You are still the boss on the bandstand Bolden, and it's your band. I want all of you to know that while I am blowing my lips off to make you famous Bolden, and you popular, Bottley, and you rich, Poree, I am losing money at the green table. Because I can shuffle the cards once and make more than a week's salary at Lincoln Park. So before we leave, let's get an understanding about the future. Bolden, will you be there or won't you?'

"Bolden says, 'Thank you Dusen, I'll be there. On time.'

"Dusen says, pointing to Poree and my brother, 'Do y'all hear that? I mean what the King is saying?'

Bottley and Poree nod their heads saying, 'Yes.' Then they shake hands. Dusen then says, 'Bolden, please try and remember to be at Lincoln Park on time, because without you there ain't no band. You are still the King. The folks still love you and Buddy Bottley. The white folks say you can't cut no more hair, so try and get yourself together.'

"Mr. Poree says, 'Come fellows, I'll drop you home.' And

he, my brother and Dusen walk out into the street.

"I look at Bolden. He is laughing to himself as he walks to the rear. I follow him and step on that first bottle he had dropped on the floor. Bolden turns around and says, 'What's that?'

"I answer, 'That's the bottle of whisky you was drinkin' when you was blowin' your horn.'

"Bolden says slowly with much surprise, 'Blowin' my horn? I wasn't blowin' my horn.'

"I said, 'Sure you were, because I was listening at you from the outside. What was you playin'?'

"Bolden says, 'Dudey, I haven't touched my baby since last week.' I thought a moment and said, softly, 'Maybe so. Maybe it was my imagination.'

"Bolden says, 'Dudey, go git some girls so we can have a party.'

"I say, 'It's late in the morning. All the girls have gone home.'

"Bolden looks at me and says, seriously, 'Dudey, go to the tonks and tell the girls Bolden is lonesome and wants to have a party, a private party. I have plenty whisky and I'm gonna blow my horn real pretty. Go find Dusen. And find Renza. Tell Renza git some girls. Let's have a shakedown. I'm so lonesome.'

"I look at the big, velvet living room chair Bolden was sitting in when I was outside peeping through the keyhole and there is his horn. I say, 'King, there is your horn.'

"Bolden says, 'Where?'

"I say, 'In the big chair.'

"Bolden says, 'Oh yeah, that's my baby.' He walks over and picks up his horn, smiles and kisses it, then puts it to his lips as he slowly relaxes in the soft chair. As he sits down he bites his lips, rubs them and says to me, 'Dudey, where's the whisky?'

"So I find the bottle and hand it to him. He drinks too much in one swallow. It spills on him and the horn. He waves the bottle to me. I drink and sit on the bed, watching him as he searches his lip with the mouthpiece for his favourite blowing position. I watch closely as he takes a long, deep breath and blows in the horn. Nothing comes out but a helpless, flabby sound. I say, 'King, what was that music you was blowing on your horn when Poree, Dusen and my brother knocked on the door?'

"Bolden says, 'I don't remember.'

"I say, 'It was a blues and the church, mixed up together.'

"Bolden says, 'It couldn't have been.'

"I say, 'You was sitting in the chair.'

"Then Bolden put his horn to his lips and started blowing something. I saw his hat and put it on the bell of his horn. I picked up the bottle and drank some whisky and listened as Bolden started playing that same blues and hymn mixed up together. I looked at the horn, at Bolden's slow moving fingers and his closed eyes. I got real scared again, hearing that music and I slowly walked out of that house through the barber shop. I opened the door, walked down the steps and up the street, because I just did not want to hear when Bolden stopped playing that mixed up music on the hymn for the Lord or the blues for the devil.

"Yes, that was first time I ever left King Bolden all alone in his home and barber shop. When I left before there was always a happy crowd, plenty of women and men, all having a good time. If that blues and hymn mixture had not scared me, I would have stayed with King Bolden and looked out for him, 'cause he was all alone without a friend in this world. That is almost the last time I saw Bolden in New Orleans.

"Walking away from Bolden's house, I soon got to thinking about Frankie Dusen. I would watch the band each time they played, because I was there, though I was not personally familiar with Dusen, as he wasn't a man to be friendly with people. I noticed that he was a serious person. Lorenzo Staulz was the only man who could make Dusen laugh. That Dusen was tall and good looking, and his straight jet-black air was parted at the side. It was long in front and it hung down on the side of his face. Women used to stand in front of the band and look at Dusen. When he looked at them they would smile nicely at him, but he'd just look back at them with a straight face and he never did return a smile. That would sorta embarrass those women. I did not like to see him do that, because even a dog deserves a smile. For that reason, especially, I was not too fond of Dusen, yet it was nice how he told

Bolden he was still boss of the band.

"But the people of Lincoln Park would never hear Bolden's horn again.

"That little meeting at Bolden's shop was on a Monday night and the next day, Tuesday, Bolden went across the river to Algiers, Louisiana, to play a funeral for a deceased member of the Young Friends of Honor Society. He was playing with Henry Red Allen Sr.'s Algiers Brass Band. The funeral started at one p.m., and it was a hot summer's day, especially around noon time. It was particularly hot for those who were marching in that broiling sun, and in a funeral march which is dead slow. The dead man had lived in Algiers and the funeral services were held there, but he was buried in the adjoining town of Gretna, a distance of about three miles.

"As is the custom, the band and society members would march the three miles slowly, playing hymns and dirges. When a hymn was finished, they would walk slightly faster, and then slow down again for the next dirge. After the dead member is buried, his family leaves the cemetery, followed by the society members, the band and the large second line. Generally, if there is not too much screaming and moaning at the graveside, the family and relatives leave immediately. When the procession has left the cemetery, the Grand Marshall looks up and down the street to see if the funeral cortege is gone and is out of sight and earshot. This he does to avoid a show of disrespect to the family of the deceased. They are in mourning, but the music the band plays next is happy and exciting music.

"So the society would respectfully and dutifully bury their late brother, in the tradition. There have been many before him, and the crowd at the graveyard knows there will be many more to come.

"Then the band and the society members line up. The snare drummer rolls a march beat and the taps. The Grand Marshall starts the march. They walk one block from the graveyard in respect. In the meantime the rough leader of the second line will have lined up his own gang. The second line leader keeps a sharp eye on the Grand Marshall to see him give the sign, a wave of the arm, to the bandleader to strike up the band.

"The bullies who lead this second line are known to all the Grand Marshalls of all the societies. There is a secret rivalry between the uniformed Marshall and the ragged ruffian. The ruffian and his bunch are determined to outdance, prance and strut the Marshall and the society members.

"The Marshall gives the bandleader the sign. Then the bass drummer strikes the big bass drum and the cornet starts *The Saints* or *Didn't He Ramble*, before the exciting three mile march back to Algiers and the hall where the society holds its meetings. The large procession now marches briskly and the band members get their kicks playing as loudly as they want.

"The Grand Marshall is in his glory; he is in the lead and the band and society follow wherever he goes. If he feels like it he will take another route, passing his home part of town, his favorite bar or the bandleader's house. The procession is no longer a funeral. Now it is a happy parade.

"Everyone is happy, but the older members of the society and the band tire easily. The ruffians in that second line are out of their minds, having a ball, dancing. The Marshalls have a tricky way of fooling those second liners. The Marshall will pretend that he is turning a corner and naturally the ruffians marching abreast of him will turn, followed by their mob. When they march on, the Marshall will suddenly whirl and strut in the opposite direction. Since the second liners are generally so excited by the music and dance with their eyes closed, only the sudden fading of the music stops them. Then comes the mad scramble of another formation abreast of the Marshall and the society. The ruffian with his big stick goes into action again, waving his followers into position.

"When the ruffian has reorganized his followers, the Marshall will look at him and laugh. 'I tricked you, you simple so-and-so.'

"As the parade passes the bar-rooms and the neighborhood of the deceased brother, the general comment to be heard, as the older folks shake their heads, is 'Well, they done put old such-and-such away.' Everybody knows that in a few days this scene will be repeated. Who is next, nobody knows, but everybody would like to be put away in the same fashion.

"During the march back, some other ruffians, tougher than the bully who leads the second line, might decide to take the stick and lead for the last few blocks to the hall, and that is when the fight starts. Neither bully wants to be embarrassed or humiliated in front of so many people, and so suddenly there is a furious street brawl. The band marches on, as there is much excitement, yelling, running, head whipping.

"The Marshall laughs, because for the last few blocks of the march, he alone is the center of attraction. His rival, the ruffian, is busy protecting his simple head, chasing someone or being chased.

"In the past, Bolden had played many parades and funerals with the Henry Allen Brass Band, which was considered amongst the best in the New Orleans area. He reported on time, shook hands with Henry Allen and then put the band's marches on the lyre on his cornet. The band marched from the hall to the home of the deceased member; they played one or two marches. From there, the funeral marched to the church where the services were held. The band waited outside the church until the long service was over. The Grand Marshall gets his signal from the undertaker to get ready for the long three mile march to Gretna.

"As the coffin is slowly carried out of the church, the band plays *What a Friend We Have in Jesus*. This is one of the three most serious scenes of the day. The first is when the dead man is carried out of his home for the last time. There is generally much crying and moaning. The second is when the body has been blessed and is being carried out of the church: much crying here. And finally, when the dead person has been buried, gone from the world forever. Each time a serious hymn or dirge is slowly played, strict to the notes, the slower the better.

"While playing the dirge, Bolden's horn screamed out a few bars of *Didn't He Ramble*. This is usually a solemn quiet time, with everyone standing in the strictest silence, respectful of God first and then of the dead. The sound of *Didn't He Ramble* is unthought of at such a time.

"All those assembled look in the direction of the band. The

horn is pushed from Bolden's lips and Mr. Allen says 'Shhhh!' Buddy, who holds his horn by his side, now bows his head and marches along. After the dirge is played and the marchers have speeded up their pace, the musicians turn to look at Bolden and to wonder what made him scream *Didn't He Ramble*. Bolden has to be helped along during the brisk march. He is very tired and the sun is hot and scorching. After about three blocks of marching the band slows down and plays another dirge, *Just a Closer Walk With Thee*. Buddy Bolden does not start to read the music on his lyre but when the band is in the most serious part of the dirge he slowly lifts his horn and screams out again *Didn't He Ramble*. The band members are shocked.

"Henry Allen takes Bolden gently by the arm and out of the line of the march from the street to the sidewalk. He notices that Bolden is sick, feverish and weak and helps him to sit down by a fence on the grass, placing his horn on his lap. An old colored lady who is standing inside the fence comes out to look at Bolden and says, 'I'll look out for the poor man. Don't worry. You catch up with the band.'

"Allen tells her, 'Madam, he's Buddy Bolden. Send for the ambulance!'

"Then he rushes off to join the rest of the band who are playing without the cornet lead. The old lady and some of her neighbors open Bolden's uniform coat, his shirt and tie and bathe his brow. They call the hospital, while Henry Allen catches up with the marching band. He gives the first cornet parts from his lyre to Freddie Keppard who is playing the second parts, and tells him to lead the band before hurrying back to see about Bolden.

"When he arrives back at Bolden's side, the ambulance has arrived and the intern is carefully examining Bolden. Bolden is taken to the charity hospital, unconscious. When he is taken to the hospital he does not have his horn, his 'baby'. The old colored lady says it was there on the grass beside him, but a little raggedy white boy picked it up and ran off with it.

"My brother Buddy gets the news that Bolden is in the Charity Hospital and he, Dusen, Lorenzo and myself rush over there. When we see Bolden he is strapped in a bed. He is not violent but the doctor says 'We ain't taking no chances.' He says that they are positively sure that Bolden is insane and that he will be kept under strict observation for a week. My brother and Dusen sit by the bedside and talk to Bolden. It was a pitiful sight. Bolden seemed like he could hear what they said, but he just looked at the ceiling and said nothing. Dusen and my brother started crying and I could not hold back my tears. Lorenzo sang in Bolden's ear, very softly, 'I thought I heard Mr. Bolden shout.' But Bolden just laid there like he was deaf. A sick man in the next bed said Bolden hadn't said one word since they brought him in. He had seen Bolden's lips move like he was talking, but no sound came out. Every day, me, my brother and the band members visited the hospital, but Bolden's condition did not change.

"The next Sunday night at Lincoln Park the dance started. Dusen had hired Li'l Bunkie Johnson in Bolden's place. The band sounded almost the same, because that Li'l Bunkie could play identically like Bolden and knew all the band's songs. After the band had started exciting the large Sunday crowd I looked and saw Mr. Poree standing on the other side of the bandstand. When the band stopped the tune they were playing Poree said, 'Dusen, how's Bolden getting along?'

"Dusen stood up, mad as General Grant when he was taking possession of Richmond, Virginny, and he hollered at Poree in front of all that big crowd of people 'You no good li'l rat bastard. You got the nerve, guts, and crust to ask about that poor sick man. Why don't you go and see? Get your no-good ass off this bandstand before I break your neck!'

"Poree got scared. Dusen picked up the drummer Williams' snare drum case and threw it with all his might at Poree, who ran off the stand, through the crowd and out of Lincoln Park.

"Renza calmed Dusen down. I went to the bar and told the waiter to bring some whisky to the band, which he did in a hurry. The band members were all mad at Poree; so mad they did not play for an hour. Dusen said to my brother when he arrived, 'Buddy, I'm quitting this joint whether Bolden comes back or not, because if I don't, I'll end up murdering that rat bastard Poree.'

"My brother said, 'We'll go over to Johnson or Jefferson

Park and let Poree see who'll draw the crowds here after we leave.'

"Two weeks after Bolden was taken to the Charity Hospital, the doctors decided they would send him to the insane asylum. Me, my brother and most of the band were there when they dressed Bolden and put him in the hospital van that took him to the Louisiana State Hospital for the Insane at Jackson, Louisiana. The date was June 5, 1907, and I'll never forget that awful day. While the orderlies dressed him, Bolden seemed completely helpless, like a baby. They had to take their time with each piece of clothing. My brother, Dusen, Lorenzo, Williams and myself all tried to strike up a conversation, but Bolden knew nobody. He was in a daze. Half alive and half asleep. He seemed to know what was going on around him, but he couldn't get his head clear, or have any reasoning power.

"After they had put his clothes on, they carefully lifted him from the side of the bed. He stood up and slowly walked, looking up at the ceiling. My brother started to cry as he walked beside Bolden. He must have asked Bolden a hundred times, 'Bolden, this is Buddy Bottley, don't you remember me? I'm your best friend.'

Bolden never answered; it seemed as if he did not hear a word. He walked out of the Charity Hospital and stepped up into the van. The van slowly pulled off and drove to Jackson.

"I went to the hospital at Jackson with my brother twice to see Buddy and each time they brought him out to the visiting room he just sat there saying nothing, just looking and smiling now and then. My brother continued to visit Bolden from time to time, because he figured that maybe Bolden's mind would snap back into the world of reality. That never happened. When I saw Bolden he was nice, fat and healthy. The officials said he was a harmless patient and there was a chance he might suddenly come to his senses.

"After all that trouble at Lincoln Park, I stopped going there and eventually became a seaman. I travelled all over the world. My brother, Dusen, Lorenzo, Williams and Poree are all dead and gone now, and Lincoln Park is gone down in history, just a memory of the good old days."

I thanked Mr. Dude Bottley for the story of his brother and Buddy Bolden, of Dusen, Poree and Lincoln Park.

"Young man," he said, "I am glad that you are going to write about these people and those days, and if you want some more interesting facts come and see me any time and I'd be more than glad to accommodate you."

I said, "Mr. Dude, when Bolden's band was so popular, were there any other cornet players around who would battle Bolden?"

"Yes," he said. "There were plenty other cornet players who could play and as I have told you before, Bolden's band had their own style and rhythm and tempo. By playing together so long, they played like a perfect machine. Each man had his notes and played his separate part of the song. There were other bands that popped up at different times but they was all highly respectful of Bolden's band because he was the King. They all respected the King.

"There was the Superior Band led by Billy Morand. There was Claiborne Williams' band from Donaldsonville. They played against Bolden many times, but Bolden cut them down. Now here's some of the cornet players who were real good: but Bolden was the boss!

There were George Moret, Andrew Kimball, Edward Clem, Dan Desdune, Wild Bill Pennington and his brother John Pennington, Wooden Joe, Freddie Keppard and little cheeky Black Bunkie Johnson. He was the closest to playing like Bolden because he would play with Bolden. He was like Bolden's protege.

"Sometimes on the stand he would get besides himself when there was a big crowd. There would be so many beautiful fine-built, full-bosomed, big-legged pretty women just waiting for the opportunity to present itself whereby they could catch Bolden's eye and wink at him. Li'l Bunkie Johnson wanted to be just like Bolden. Bolden liked Bunkie and would sit with his horn on his lap and let Bunkie do the blowing. Yes, he loved to hear Li'l Bunkie play, 'cause Bunkie had copied his style note for note. When he blowed he held his horn up and stood just like Bolden did, looking up to the sky. He even had the big white handkerchief to wipe his lips and forehead, just like Bolden."

"Mr. Dude," I asked, "Why did you say that Bunk Johnson was cheeky?"

He said, "Well, you see, Bunkie, in my honest opinion, was cheeky because he got to thinking he was better than Bolden. Many people believed that he was better than the King. I used to stand by the bandstand and watch every move he made. He wanted to be King, because he would play all of Bolden's solos and then add other notes of his own, which I must give him credit for because they sounded good. When he did that, all the men of the band would look at him.

"On Monday nights, all the District underworld whores and pimps would come out to the park. Bolden would be invited over to their tables and he'd leave the bandstand to go and ball it up with the pretty downtown Creole whores. Bunkie would take over when Bolden was gone. Yes, Li'l Bunkie would blow and blow, just like the King. That's when he'd play his favorite tune which made the crowd scream and holler for him to play it over. He'd tell Lorenzo when to announce the tune, and Lorenzo would stand up, the drummer would roll the snare and everyone would quiet down and listen to Lorenzo as he hollered: 'Now, ladies and gentlemens and rats and cats, and all the other wild animals gathered here on this great occasion! The great little Bunkie Johnson will now render his classical sonata *The Whore's Gone Crazy*.

"Everyone would get hysterical and raise up some hell: clapping whistling and screaming. Lorenzo would motion for them to calm down and then Bunkie would start blowing that tune. It was a real, lowdown, funky blues, very slow, and everyone danced. This lasted for about twenty minutes. Yes, they just shook and rubbed bellies, not moving four foot apiece while Bunkie played the whole tune.

"That was something to see. That big crowd, their shoulders and heads barely moving but the lower portions of their bodies shaking and wriggling like a barrel of rattle snakes. Bunkie would really blow that blues and the huge crowd would be all out of breath from doing all that shaking and belly rubbing. When the blues were over the band would leave the stand to go and join the women. Bunkie would join his bunch of women, coming on like Bolden the King.

"When the dance ended I would watch him leave the place with a half dozen black strumpets following him. One would hold his horn, one his hat, one his coat, so he made his departure just like the King, with a crowd. He reminded me of that old saying: 'Monkey see, monkey do!'

"Now there was only one other cornet player who could make the King take notice and that was the Creole from downtown, Manuel Perez. He could and would blow. Things would get real tense when Robichaux would hire him in his band over on the dicty pavilion. He would be blowing, and now and then he'd blow one of the King's songs. But John Robichaux would not let him extend himself because the pavilion was full of high class folks. When Perez would blow out, Bolden and the band would laugh. The King would say, ' Listen at the Frenchman! Sounds like he's raring to go, but old John won't let him 'cause he knows the King is over heah!'

"That Li'l Bunkie Johnson was something. Lots of folks thought he was Bolden's little brother. Some even called him young Bolden. Some called him the Prince (the King's son). He sho' could consume some alcohol and he had credit liquor bills in every joint in New Orleans. He was an attraction wherever he went. He would play his cornet anywhere. People in the bar-rooms would say, 'Bunkie, play like the King!' and then he'd play his horn standing by the bar just like Bolden the King. He would have dozens of glasses of all kinds of drinks before him and he would drink every last one of them. I used to see him every place, him and his horn. I'd see him at night, in the early morning, in the evening, 'round twilight as well as at midday, midnight, all the time. It was a mystery to me: when did Li'l Bunkie sleep? He was a tough hard piece of meat, How he did not drop dead from gallivanting was a wonder!"

I said to Mr. Bottley, "You've been so nice to tell me all this about your brother and Buddy Bolden, and Bunk and all. Can I treat you or give you a few dollars?"

Mr. Dude Bottley replied, "No son. I don't need nothing. I'm so glad to see that some Negro is interested in writing a story so that the people will remember the great Bolden and Lincoln Park, and what the good old days were like."

2
The Last Days of Storyville

At lunchtime at Cookshop's restaurant I heard all sorts of fantastic tales of the District's characters. Here's the story of New Orleans' most famous Negro ladies' man, his woman Ready Money, and their clever departure from that city.

For about fifteen years (1900 to 1915), the District's most highly respected ladies' man was Bob Rowe. Bob was a tall man, about six feet, sort of slim and raw-boned, considered tall, brown and handsome. As a young man he was asked and begged to become the pimp of an old wise streetwalker, Warmbody Stell. She hustled and supported Bob for quite a few years. Stell was a hop head and a consumptive. Eventually, Bob took up with another fast woman named Ready Money, because Warmbody Stell had become a problem and a nuisance. She went to jail with a sentence of three months. Bob heard her many pleas to get her out but he ignored them all and let her die in the Parish Prison. Bob rarely smiled or joked. He was, as the underworld would say, cold-blooded and heartless.

The renowned Tom Anderson was the king of the white tenderloin and Bob Rowe was king of the Negro tenderloin. He was the unofficial czar of the District and everybody respected him as such. He was loved and supported by Ready Money, who eventually became the District's most famous Negro madame during that period. Ready Money was a small woman, real light colored. She had big blue eyes and yellow hair and could easily have "jumped the fence," that is, passed for white. She came to New Orleans from the Cajun country. After hustling most of the big name brothels, she opened her own. She lived up to her name because it was the custom of the smart boys when losing at games of chance to call or send a stooge to their women and get them some more gambling money.

On occasions when Mr. Rowe's luck at the gambling table deserted him he would call or send a message, "Go tell Ready Money send me some fresh cash," which never failed to arrive.

During that period and for many more years (between 1900 and 1935,) the Big Twenty Five, a gambling house and bar, was the District's number one spot. It was the hangout of all the wise boys of that period. Sporting women came by after work to relax, drink and give their earnings to their men. It was the headquarters and clearing house of most of the action in the District.

The District's most beloved pimp was Clerk Wade, the younger brother of Louie Wade who was called the Professor. Louie, for many years, played the piano at Lulu White's Mahogany Hall. Clerk Wade is still talked about in New Orleans today by the old timers who are still around. As the story goes, Louie Wade, who had made a lot of money playing piano in the famous brothels, went to visit his folks who lived below the city in a small village called Violet, Louisiana. When he returned to the city he brought back with him his younger brother, Clerk, who was about eighteen years old. Louie got Clerk a job waiting tables at Tom Anderson's Arlington Café.

During Mr. Anderson's reign as King of the New Orleans Tenderloin he owned, at different times, the Stage, the Arlington Café and the Arlington Annex. Mr. Anderson, wealthy, and tired of his notorious reputation and livelihood, sadly spoke these wards of warning to all who sought this protection and advice:

> "The handwriting is on the wall. The District is through. The suckers and fools are wising up and everybody who earned a dollar by hook or crook had better square up. The tricks ain't walking and the Johns are squawking."

From time to time, the highly honored and respected Tom Anderson would send forth an order:

> Mr. Anderson says, "Close all the houses 'til the heat's off!"
> Mr. Anderson says, "No gambling, the police's gonna raid all the joints!"
> Mr. Anderson says, "Don't open until he gives the word, ok?"

It was obeyed instantly by Pete Lala, Johnny Lala, Fewclothes, Spano and all the others. White dives and black dives alike. Doors were locked and all lights put out and the joints were abandoned and deserted. Anderson would get the news that the police were about to crack down on the District and he would relay the word to Pete Lala who, in turn, told George Fewclothes, Frank Early, Johnny Lala, Spano, and Ludlow and in an hour or so all the owners of the joints in the underworld obeyed the warning and sat pat until Anderson sent word that the heat was off and they could resume business.

During the time I played in New Orleans in some of the notorious joints, I had the opportunity to witness what happened during these lulls of activity. The command from on high when obeyed caused a stop of business. Gamblers did not gamble, the register in the bar-rooms did not jingle, the tricks stopped walking and everyone became sullen and angry. The bands in the joints just sat around, they rarely played. The bartender sat silently or went to sleep. Not a mouse stirred. And at such times you would hear the city officials and the police discussed in the most contemptible and uncouth manner. This was because the people of the underworld, no matter how rotten or illegitimate their method of living was, all felt that for some reason they were justified in their practises and professions.

I would hear speeches from the owners, the waiters, the bartenders, musicians, cooks, and even some crooked policemen who were missing their grant and payoffs:

> "The Mayor is a sonofabitch!"
> "The District Attorney is a lying bastard!"
> "The Chief of Police is a two-faced stinking rat!"
> "The detectives are a bunch of no good...."
> "The Mayor is a lying, no good, two-faced bastard. Before that poor raggedy sonofabitch was elected, he promised us that everything would go on peacefully and that the District would be kept wide open. Now he ain't been in office but four months and he's acting worse than that other lying bastard that was in office before! And that other stinking bastard, the Governor, up in Baton Rouge, got his hand in the pot! He wants

his rakeoff. That sonofabitch who's putting the pressure on the Mayor and them rat bastards in the first precinct! I pay one captain to lay off and two hours later here comes another bastard from out of some other precinct demanding that I give him some money...and you got to give it to them."

"Before he got elected, when I gave him my money to help him with his campaign, that lying-ass Mayor swore on his dead mother that we'd have peace and prosperity. Now look what happens."

"I was at the City Hall when the Mayor was inaugurated and sworn in. I looked right straight in that bastard's mouth when he swore and put his dirty greasy hands on the Bible and said that he promised to be a good Mayor. Later I went to the Inaugural Ball as an invited guest because some of my money paid for that. He pulled me aside and told me confidentially that the good days were right round the corner. We even drank a toast of champagne, which my money bought. And now he's in office, he'll speak to no one, and if you set foot near his office them rotten police will lock you up. Do you call that gratitude?"

Tom Anderson's club was the favorite hangout of big wheels of New Orleans' underworld. Clerk's cool, calm, efficient manner of waiting tables and serving the guest without mistakes or complaints caught the eye of the head waiter, a friend of Louie Wade. The head waiter promoted Clerk to serve the number one station, which was always reserved for Mr. Anderson and his important friends and their wives, women and girlfriends. Clerk worked this job for a couple of years as Mr. Anderson's personal waiter. Nightly as he stood at attention, four or five feet off from the view of the high class guests of Tom Anderson, he watched their polite manners and behavior and silently listened and heard all sorts of tales, problems, plans and underworld strategy discussed. He copied and practiced the manners and actions of these smart men and noticed all of the things that annoyed these guests, especially the women. He especially patterned his manners and public behaviour after Mr. Anderson, who was always immaculate, cool headed and calm, no matter what story was related to him. Mr. Anderson rarely smiled or laughed, and when he did it was with restraint, never loud or hilariously. No matter what Mr. Anderson listened to, whether it was comedy or tragedy, he always reacted as if he had heard the story before.

Clerk especially noticed that Mr. Anderson was extra polite to all the women, even the ones who had too much to drink. He listened to their love problems, when their men were there and when these women came in alone. Clerk heard Mr. Anderson repeat these words of counsel hundreds of times: "Take it easy! Everything will turn out for the better. Don't do nothing drastic; you may regret it."

Clerk heard many beautiful and expensively dressed women sit for hours with Tom Anderson and plead with him to be their man, advise them in business, have affairs with them and not once did Clerk hear Tom Anderson agree or accept their love or proposition. Many a time after these women were escorted outside to a taxi and Mr. Anderson returned and passed Clerk on his way into his office, he would softly say to Clerk: "Clerk, women are very funny animals, aren't they?"

Clerk always softly replied, "They sure are, Mr. Anderson."

Mr. Anderson was well aware that Clerk, from his respectful distance, had heard their conversations and he also noticed that Clerk attended to his business and only spoke when spoken to. He never joked or kidded with the other help, waiters, bartenders or cooks. He was punctual, neat and alert. Just about the perfect waiter. But Clerk's job at the Arlington came to an end on a Sunday morning about four a.m. when a fine party came in and sat at Clerk's station. They were two men and three women. The five people were more drunk than sober and very loud to the point of annoyance to the other guests. Clerk seated them and stood by with his pad and pencil in hand, waiting for their order. One of the men said, "Boy, bring us a bottle of champagne and a bottle of bourbon."

Clerk brought the two bottles and a set up of ice and soda. He poured their drinks and then stepped off to his usual position and stood at attention, looking off in another direction but now and then looking at the table and the noisy party. The party of five were paired off into twos and an extra woman. The two couples drank and talked and kidded each other. The single woman drank the bourbon, spilling more on the table than she poured into the small glass with her unsteady hand. She said to the two couples, very angrily, "I'm sick and tired of waiting for that sonofabitch. We were all supposed to come out and have some fun and he calls me and says he can't make it. It's always some excuse. I know he's with some other bitch. I know I'll get me another bastard. I'll try something different for a change. I have jazzed a Chinaman and jazzed a Mexican. I jazzed a savage Indian. I've got one more to go and that is jazz a nigger, and then I will have gone around the world."

Looking up at Clerk she yelled: "Oh! There's a nigger! A nice, brown, clean nigger. Hey nigger! Come here. Let me see you. Let me get a good look at you. Maybe I'll let you jazz me this morning."

Clerk looked straight ahead as if he did not hear her. The woman's loud and vulgar talk drew all the guests' attention, also the attention of the bartenders, waiters and other help. Somebody went to the rear office of Tom Anderson and he quickly and calmly approached the wild party. Colored maids who worked in white brothels related how white whores all knew how to make their pimps raving and violently furious by yelling when arguing and fighting: "I'm going over in coontown and get me a nigger pimp!"

That remark made a white pimp wreck a mansion to splinters and whip a whore damn near to death. All the mansions and brothels employed Negro maids. A maid, when the battles were raging, would at times come out and go into the bar-rooms and tell about the fights. There was always lots of laughter when she said: "One of them crazy whores told her pimp she was coming over here and get her a nigger pimp."

When Mr. Anderson hurried out of his office and to the drunken woman he told Clerk, softly, "Take the rest of the night off."

Then he pulled up a chair and sat next to the woman. Clerk went to the dressing room, took off his white waiter's jacket, put on his hat and walked out of Anderson's and walked over to the Big Twenty Five. On his slow walk to Big Twenty Five, which was two blocks away, Clerk thought about how the white men at the tale with the drunken woman had been silent, stopped drinking and stared angrily at the raving woman and then at Clerk. Clerk also recalled how the other colored waiters and the white bartenders had stood about at their stations with deadpan expressions and bulging eyes, also that everybody had relaxed when Mr. Anderson walked from his office and sat at the wild party's table. He remembered too that when he put on his coat and hat and passed the waiters and bartenders no one spoke a word to him.

When Clerk stepped into Big Twenty Five he looked about the place and the scene was very happy in a quiet sort of way. Clerk would also stop at Big Twenty Five after he finished his work at the Arlington at about six or seven o'clock in the morning. He worked seven nights a week, from seven to seven. If business was slow at Arlington Café, one of the waiters would leave an hour earlier in relays. Usually, when Clerk entered Big Twenty Five the revelers were tired, drunk and about ready to leave for their homes. That scene bored him. But the scene he saw this night was interesting because the people were still full of life, many beautiful fast women and well-dressed men having a good time. He sat in a booth, ordered a bottle of beer and watched the festivities. Clerk sat in the booth alone, because the other times he had come to Big Twenty Five it was near daybreak and the folks were either drunk or tired and uncommunicative, so he knew very few of the patrons personally. He would also be tired, having listened to a lot of chatter all night. The scene was boring and his main reason for stopping there after work was to see his older brother, Louie Wade, who would come in after he had finished playing the piano in one of the famous mansions of Lulu White, Gypsy Shaeffer or other madames.

This particular morning Clerk watched the scene and silently waited until his brother entered the place.

When Louie walked in, a party called him to their table and ordered a drink for him. Then Louie sat at the piano and played.

After a while he looked around and saw Clerk. He stepped from the piano and joined Clerk in the booth, while Clerk told him of the incident at Tom Anderson's.

Louie told Clerk, "Forget about the job at the Arlington Café. I'll get you a waiter's job here. Do you have any money saved?"

Clerk said, "Yes. I've saved fifteen-hundred dollars since I've been working at Tom Anderson's."

Louie spoke to the owner of the Big Twenty Five and Clerk started waiting tables there.

Louie was very fond of his younger brother and taught him very quickly the tactics and strategy of dealing with the women of the District. Clerk listened and learned. Clerk was of medium height, slim and delicate physically. He was nice looking, smooth, brown and possessed two piercing shining black eyes. The old timers say he spoke so softly that you barely heard him. When in a conversation with him the other person asked continually, "What did you say, Clerk?"

Maybe it was a trick Clerk used because during the brief time he worked at Big Twenty Five as a waiter, the guests were always asking, "What did you say, waiter?"

Then he would lean over and again answer them softly. It wasn't long before one of the landladies fell for Clerk and told him to get out of that waiter's uniform and come with her. The woman's name was Patti Smith. She was one of the top madames. In a little while Clerk had the largest wardrobe in the District, a cigar box full of jewelry and diamonds, and a reputation of never wearing the same suit more than twice. He had so many clothes he had to hire a valet to keep them in order. During his career he kept a half dozen characters well dressed with his cast-off clothing. At the height of his reign as number one ladies' man in the District he had six sporting women sharing his affections peacefully. He was never known to have an argument, never heard talking loud or in a heated argument with anyone. He never had any hassle with his women and did not tolerate any argument or abuse from his women. If one of them got loud and out of line, the others dragged her away from him. Clerk's popularity and notoriety spread until his name and fame were the talk of all the underworld. Everyone connected with the tenderloin talked and discussed Clerk and his soft talk and the obedience of his women, and of the women who showered him with gifts.

Women proposed to him, men and women flocked to Big Twenty Five just to see him, to watch him stand at the bar or sit down to eat. Clerk, daily and nightly, received sealed letters, packages and notes from women which contained money, jewelry, clothes. In spite of New Orleans being a Southern city there was a close alliance between the white and colored District fraternities. It was said and verified that a few white whores and madames sent Clerk money and presents by their professors, maids and servants. Clerk was like a god. Everybody loved him. When he walked the streets of the District the children followed him. His soft voice and genteel manner captivated everyone.

It was the custom of the police to whip, kick and brutalize the young pimps when they were arrested and locked up for vagrancy, loitering and having no visible means of support, but for some reason, (I guess they too were charmed by Clerk's manner,) they were very tender with him. He replied to a judge who was rebuking him: "Judge, your honor, I swear I've never in my life asked or demanded any money from a woman. They just give it to me. Sometimes when I refuse it they jam it down my pocket."

Clerk was good to all the boys when they were down on their luck. They could always get a few dollars or could go to the lunch counter at Twenty Five and get a meal on Clerk's bill.

There were scores of light colored mulatto sporting women who worked or hustled as white and most of them, if they did not pass for white or have white pimps, came by Twenty Five after work to relax, drink and hear the gossip. There was a racket that was very embarrassing to the young pimps, hustlers, gamblers and sports. There was a group of notorious bad men, bullies and hogs as they were called. These men were rough characters who preyed on the young smart boys. When not in jail for some crime, they hung out in the popular joints in the District, picking

61

fights and threatening the moneyed boys if they did not pay them protection money. If they were ignored or refused the boys were waylaid and beaten. The leaders of these roughnecks were Aaron Harris, Boar Hog, Steel Arm Johnny, Fay Boy, Rough Nuts, Knock on the Wall, Raw Head, Sneekers and dozens of others. They beat the smart boys and if they still were not paid off, they waylaid their women and beat them. When Clerk took off the waiter's uniform he was threatened by a bully named Ceaphus. Clerk's woman heard about it. Ceaphus was found in an empty lot with his throat cut from ear to ear. Clerk was never annoyed again.

Clerk listened to the pleas of a beautiful young fiery-tempered prostitute to take her in his stable. When a pimp possessed more than two women who gave him their earnings, the women were referred to as women of so and so's stable. Also whores were commonly called mud kickers, (like a swift race horse – a swift woman.) In the underworld a smart, shrewd, fast sporting woman who is intelligent, with no weaknesses, habits (dope) is highly prized and respected. She is the lily of the valley.

Clerk told this girl if she would cut out her tantrums and act more dignified when around the joints and especially in his presence, he might consider spending some time with her when he was not busy. She begged and begged him to let her tell the District that he was her man, which was the custom in those days. Successful ladies' men were at a premium, they were kept busy by their stables of women and were particular about corralling stray whores because they were a nuisance and meant jail, fighting, drinking, dope, ignorance, uncleanliness. First class ladies' men and first class whores were very particular of who they took up with. One could be caused lots of trouble.

So the class system prevailed. You stayed in your class and social level. Clerk listened to her pleas and consented to be her man as long as she behaved herself. But this was a wild, frantic Creole girl. She was very mixed up blood-wise: part French, part Italian, part Indian and a small portion of Zulu blood flowed in her veins. When she got drunk that mixed blood boiled within her and she would become very melancholy, grieving about the low, degrading life she lived. One night Clerk and the pimps had taken their stables of women to the Roof Garden to hear King Oliver's Band and to let the women get some fresh air, a welcome relief from the confinement of their brothels and cribs. Clerk told Angelina, as she was called, that she could not come because she was not presenting him with the quota of money that she swore she would give him weekly. He said to her very softly, "Little girl, it costs a whole lot of money to be Mr. Clerk Wade's woman."

The hot burning tears streamed down Angelina's pretty rouged cream colored cheeks. She cried and cried and cried and nothing could stop her. Clerk and his stable and the other pimps and their stables left for the Roof Garden; they left the Big Twenty Five laughing and in high spirits. Angelina sat at the table in a booth crying and drinking absinthe. Her sobs annoyed the other customers and the gamblers in the rear. Everybody tried to stop her sobbing; they consoled her but she never stopped crying. Big Twenty Five took on an atmosphere of an undertaker's parlor; no one could remember when a woman had cried so long and so hard. The owner escorted her out on the sidewalk and walked her up the street so the customers could get some relief. He came back in the place and said, "That's a bad sign, a woman crying like that."

After about an hour Angelina returned to Twenty Five, sat in the booth, and resumed her crying but not as loud as before but with deep sad sobs.

She ordered drink after drink of absinthe till late in the morning. She sat watching the door. When daylight shone through the swinging doors, she was still watching. She heard a lot of laughter and in walked the happy crowd of the District's elite: Morris Moore and his stable, Chinee Morris and his stable, Emile Pierre and his stable, Sam Depass and his stable, and in walked Clerk, behind the crowd because he hated noise and notoriety.

After the ball they had gone to Pratt's Café and had a big breakfast. Clerk must not have eaten because one of his women said to the waiter, "Bring my daddy a pork chop sandwich, cooked nice and brown and crisp."

The frivolity was suddenly broken by Angelina's crying and

sobs. The place became quiet as the revelers looked in the direction of the wails. Somebody told Clerk to go and console Angelina. So he goes over to the booth and sits next to her. After a while the waiter brings the pork chop sandwich. Clerk picked up the sandwich and raised it to his mouth. Angelina took a snub nosed pistol from her purse and emptied the bullets into Clerk's chest. She shot him five times; he toppled over and down to the floor. Clerk Wade moaned these words as he weakened from the hot burning lead in his chest, "Lord have mercy on my soul."

The crowd screamed and there was panic. Angelina laid the gun on the table, placed her head on the table and cried again. The pimps put out the fire that was on Clerk's chest, caused by the fire of the gun at such close range. They took Clerk's shoes off. One of them kneeled down besides Clerk and he was heard to say, "Li'l girl, I'm sorry I did not take you to the ball."

Clerk died and that was that.

Angelina was arrested but released after she told the judge her side of the tragedy. The District was like a graveyard when the news spread that Clerk was dead. They laid him out three days and nights. All the madames in the District closed their establishments while Clerk reposed in state. The King was dead and gone. His funeral was the largest in the history of the District. He had sixty funeral carriages in his funeral procession pulled by horses. The District was crowded with thousands of people. Everybody of any significance went to his grave. He was taken back home to the little village of Violet. There were thousands of wreaths and floral remembrances piled on his grave. Reverend Sunshine preached a masterful eulogy, speaking of the kindness in Clerk Wade's heart. When they lowered Clerk's body in the ground his whores hollered and swore of how they would revenge his death. It was quite a problem pulling up three of them who had jumped down in the hole on top of the coffin, screaming and howling: "Bury me with him! Take me with you, Clerk! I can't live without you, Daddy."

The whores raised so much hell in the graveyard that the sheriff warned he would lock the whole funeral up in jail. It was quite a while before the District calmed down to normality. The pimps got panicky because the whores in the District all had the blues and they grieved over the passing of Clerk. Within a month, seven pimps of lesser stature to Clerk were slain by their women. The next week, Jackie Brown, a pal of Clerk, was shot by his woman at a ball. Jackie was New Orleans' leading dancing master (called an M.C. today.) He was a rival of Buddy Bottley. So many pimps were slain that the smart boys were leery of taking money from their girls. Angelina did not live long. Nobody would speak to her. The whores tricked her. They crushed a pack of sewing needles and put them in her douche bag. She was taken to the Charity Hospital in great pain and died screaming in agony. The doctors were puzzled as they did not know how to extract the sharp steel particles that were all about, deep down in her innards.

After the tragic deaths of Clerk Wade, Angelina, Jackie Brown, and a dozen other District characters, which happened in the span of one month's time, the colored section of the District was never the same again. During the slaughter of so many smart boys and girls daily there was a tension in the atmosphere. Who would be next on the death list? The madames, landladies and sporting girls changed; they were not afraid of getting beaten up and mistreated by their men if the tricks were not walking and the money was short as it had been before. They became very bold and said out loud in the joints, restaurants and dives: "If my man hits me, I'll send him to meet Clerk. I'll do like Angelina done; light his ass up like a Christmas tree or a Catholic church."

The ladies' men were very careful about disciplining their women, so they spared the rod and spoiled the child. After work, the sporting women openly withheld their money, caroused about the joints getting drunk and signifying about: "There'll be some changes made – I ain't the fool I used to be."

They openly argued in public with their men and defied them to strike them. The strict morale and iron discipline of the District disappeared. Many pimps lost their women and support. Some left town, some went to the dogs, some became bums, some went to work, some because hustlers, some went to the grave. The panic was over.

Louie Wade composed a song that became very popular. It was a slow lament: *If You Want A Stable, You Better Get You A Horse*. All the sporting women sang it, also the queers. The lament caused the smart boys to get together and seek a solution, in order to get the sporting women back in line, because they were singing "Get you a horse if you want you a stable," louder and louder.

Mr. Bob Rowe, who was the District's most respected pimp, called a meeting at Big Twenty Five and most of the noted pimps were in attendance, namely Morris Moore, Son Pennerman, Emile Pierre, Chinee Morris, Sam Depass, Louis Decuiz, Kitchen Sam, Paul Gross, Water Coolie Williams, Sweet Smelling Willie, Notoriety Rufus Brown, Sweetie Pie, Johnny "Be Kind", Sweet Honey, Diamond Chest Jimmy, Money Wasting Bob, Pretty Jack Jenkins, Bob Keno, Pretty Willie, Fancy Jack, Easy Rider, Long Goody, Dick Lee, Pretty André. But the meeting was a failure because they could not figure out a plan to discipline the whores. They argued and argued and the final solution was that the only way to keep sporting women in line was to whip them or kill them, so there were loud boasts of all manner of murder, slaughter, mayhem, brutality, then they all went to the bar and got drunk. Others left and smoked the pipe.

* * *

Bob Rowe sat in a booth alone, watching the pimps, who were all confused and in a bad mood. Most of them weren't spending their money as freely as before, because their women were holding out or freezing them out slowly. The future looked dismal for him and the boys. He got to thinking about what would happen to his race horses if Ready Money started acting up as the other whores were doing. As Mr. Rowe sat there, thinking of the past, the future and the loud boisterous threats of the pimps and their plots of murder, killing and slaughter, in walked Mr. Barrel of Fun. His name was appropriate because he was forever telling jokes, the life of any party. When he walked in and heard all the bitter chatter he yelled, surprised, "What the hell has happened?"

Nobody pays any attention to him because they are not in

the mood for joking. He looks around and sees Bob Rowe sitting in the booth. He goes over, saying "Bob, what's the trouble?"

Bob tells him seriously, "Sit down, Fun".

Barrel of Fun sits down and Bob says, "Fun, this ain't no time for no joking and kidding. The boys are mad 'cause the whores ain't acting right."

Fun says, "I hear that!"

Bob Rowe says, "It don't matter if Ready Money leaves me. I can always get other women, but I don't want to lose my six horses. You think I should try and sell them, Fun?"

Barrel of Fun says: "Hell, no! Keep them horses. Your luck will change."

The six broken-down race horses that Mr. Barrel of Fun advised Mr. Bob Rowe to keep were all of very fine breeding and culture. They were very clannish and loved to run among the crowd, content always to let another horse lead the pack and, according to the track record book, it was recorded that only on one occasion did one of his nags take the initiative to lead the pack, then dropped back to third place because it felt that it was being a show-off.

New Orleans was one of the first cities in the United States to have big time racing and Negroes played a big part as trainers, grooms, jockeys and track attendants. There were quite a few Negroes who owned and raced horses. Barrel of Fun was a noted trainer, and worked for Colonel E. R. Bradly, who owned one of America's largest stables "The Greentree" and breeding farms. Barrel of Fun loved New Orleans and was considered one of the District's most popular sports with a dollar. He and Bob Rowe were very good friends and it was he who arranged for Bob to buy horses, which he trained, other than his main job working for Bradly. Mr. Rowe's horses rarely ran in the money but he kept his small stable mainly for the notoriety he received as being a race-horse owner in the city and having his name listed in the scratch sheet of New Orleans newspapers.

After the racing season, the horses at the track were shipped to other tracks to race but Mr. Rowe's horses remained in New Orleans for the rest of the year until the season started again, which meant that Mr. Rowe had to feed and shelter his nags while they remained idle. Around the joints and gambling houses Mr. Rowe patiently boasted (when the season closed) "Wait till next year. I'll show them!"

Mr. Barrel of Fun had returned from a racing season in California and he told Bob of California's sunshine, gold and beauty. He also explained how the fresh, light California air would help his health, because at times when it rained and the cold heavy damp air settled over the city, Bob Rowe had difficulty breathing normally, a symptom of the dreaded consumption. So Mr. Rowe made plans to take his horses to California. He, Barrel of Fun, and his woman Ready Money, sat down and mapped out a plan of strategy whereby they could ship the horses to California and have a nice sum of money to tide them over until Ready Money could get her connections in California and open her a first class meat market. The police in New Orleans were making it tough for the madames and their girls to make a dollar (that is, a peaceful one.) So they spread the news and called a meeting of all the big shots in the District, the pimps, madames, whores, gamblers, hustlers, bartenders and all the owners of joints. These people believed in Bob Rowe and Ready Money because in the past their counsel was always wise. They gave a cocktail party at Pete Lala's, which was the District's number one cabaret, on a Sunday evening. Joe Oliver's band played and everyone of importance attended dressed in their finest regalia.

When the affair was just about reaching its peak, that is, everyone in a gay mood, Ready Money told Joe Oliver to play the blues real sad, which he did. Then, when the crowd returned to their seats, she had the drummer Ratty Jean Vigne, roll his snares and she pleaded sadly with tears in her big blue eyes for attention. You could hear a pin drop as she informed the gathering of the many humiliating abuses she had constantly received from the brutal police of New Orleans which they all knew so well. She then told them of her plan to organize them. This would cost money which would be paid to an official of the city government who was higher than the police department, who would see to it immediately that the police ceased molesting the madames so they could operate their houses in harmony and peace and make an honest living. She proposed that each person present come up to the table where she stood, sign their name and pledge twenty dollars as an active member, which most of them did.

She had Joe Oliver play the spiritual *Down by the Riverside* so the crowd could march up to her and rally to the cause. When the last bill was stuffed into her big purse she called upon the famous Rev. Sunshine who asked for quiet and then blessed the gathering. Then Ready Money told the the revelers, who were happy at the prospect of a new era of peace and plenty, that they would give a big ball for their treasury so that they would have a fund to help themselves in time of distress. She blew kisses to the crowd and yelled, "We'll show them goddamned police!"

Everybody screamed, yelled and clapped their hands and they balled till the next morning to the music of Joe Oliver. During the following week, placards and tickets appeared in the District, which read thusly:

The First Grand Ball and Soirée to be given at the Economy Hall
May 2, 1919, by the
HELPING HAND BENEVOLENT AID AND PROTECTIVE
ASSOCIATION

Organized on April 7, 1919, for the aid and protection of sick, needy, helpless, disabled, aged and persecuted Sporting girls and Madames who are confined to hospitals, pest houses, houses of correction, criminal institutions, jails and penitentiaries.

Officers

Black Sis: President	Ready Money: Treasurer
Rotten Rosie: Vice President	Ida Jackson: Ex Officio
Mollie Hatcher: Secretary	Lily the Crip: Delegate
Mary Meathouse: Recording Secretary	One-Arm Edna: Sick C'ttee
Warmbody Stell: Financial Secretary	Bird Leg Nora: Trustee
Barrel of Fun: Sgt. at Arms	Bob Rowe: Director

Reverend Sunshine Money: Pastor

MUSIC FURNISHED BY JOE OLIVER'S BAND
Admission 50c. Pay at the Door

Now while the preparations for the ball were in hand, here's a little story of one of the close friends of Mr. Bob Rowe who planned to ride with him to California: Whitefolks Weber.

Weber's mother was a white woman who came to New Orleans for the races. While in New Orleans for the racing season she gave birth to a baby boy. She hired a colored woman as cook, housekeeper and wet nurse, because she spent most of her time at the races during the day and at night spots at night. The colored woman cared for the baby as if he was her own. When the racing season ended and the horses departed so did the baby's mother, but she gave the nurse a good sum of money and promised that train fare and additional money would be sent to bring the baby to her as soon as she found a house in the city where the next racing season would begin. The nurse never received one letter or message as to the whereabouts of the baby's mother. The nurse became too attached to the baby to report the mother's disappearance to the authorities and she raised the baby as her own. She lived in the section of New Orleans called the Battlefield and the battlefield it was. It was New Orleans' roughest residential section. It was noted as the field of carnage.

At an early age, as was the custom in the city, the boy was nicknamed by the neighbors: "Whitefolks". I could never find out his first name and nobody could remember him being called any other name but Whitefolks Weber. Whitefolks was raised amongst the colored folks and lived as a Negro. He never attempted to go back to his people. He grew up with young battlefield roughnecks such as Boar Hog, Rough Nuts, Black Benny, and Red Happy. He became one of the city's most noted gamblers and ladies' men.

Whitefolks, at an early age, said that the only friend he had in this cruel world was the woman who cared for him like a mother and he called her "Maw" and he respected her. He learned to hustle, gamble and get a dollar just like the other young roughnecks. His maw sent him to school neat and clean until he decided to quit. Then he promoted floating dice and card games in empty houses and lots. Whitefolks acquired the respect of all the members of New Orleans' gambling fraternity. The news spread in the District of his daring in games of chance. He gambled all over New Orleans, paid his debts and never welshed in paying losses. Whenever the police surprised Whitefolks when he ran games in lots or in an empty house he never ran as the other gamblers did, because he did not fear the police. From a safe distance, the other gamblers would watch Weber as he calmly talked to the officers and gave them some money. When the games were slow in the established gambling dens and tonks in New Orleans, the big time gamblers would journey back o' town in the battlefield in search of Weber's games.

When he was seventeen years of age, the Money Wasters, a notorious New Orleans social club, gave one of their semi-annual balls at the Co-operative Hall. Buddy Petit's band played for the affair. Weber and his gang of rowdies decided they would go to the dance so they went to the Palmer Bros. Tailors on South Rampart Street and bought long pants, box-back suits like all the notorious pimps, gamblers, hustlers and characters wore. The night of the big ball, Weber and his young friends went downtown to attend the ball which was one of the District's most publicized affairs. Everybody of any note was there, especially since Mr. Buddy Petit was playing.

Weber and his boys were the center of attraction, dressed in their brand new box-back suits, candy striped shirts, Edwin Clapp shoes and with sparkling new twenty dollar pieces on their watch fobs. The older hustlers and gamblers introduced Weber and his boys to the folks they did not know. As was the custom at balls held at the Co-operative, Economy, Globe, Perseverance and Olympia halls, the promoter would hire a pianist or small combo to play next to the bar to give the ball a cabaret atmosphere, so that when the folks finished a dance set they went to the back bar for refreshments and singing.

After twelve o'clock, tables were set off, the police were paid off and the gambling started. Dice games, poker, cotch, coon can, black jack and skin, also three card (called "miner" in New Orleans.) Weber and his boys drifted by the games and watched the proceedings. He eye-balled the dice game that was in progress, promoted by the famous Bob Rowe. Bob saw the attentive expression on Weber's face and said, "You wanna play, kid?" Weber said "Yeah," and moved close to the table. When the dice came round to Weber, Bob Rowe said, "It's your shot, kid". Weber picked up the dice, saying, "I shoot five dollars!"

His bet was accepted (that is, faded) and he slowly shuffled the dice in his hands and then rolled them. When the dice stopped Bob Rowe said, "You win, kid. The dice says 'leven."

The dice rolled and rolled and Weber never lost a bet. In a few minutes all the money was piled in front of Weber. Bob Rowe said, "Kid, you've won all the money but I got to fade you."

He took off his diamond stick pin, saying "The pin is worth five hundred. Shoot!"

Weber rolled the dice – seven! Weber picked up the pin and stuck it in his tie.

Bob took off his twenty dollar gold piece on his watch chain, saying, "Shoot!"

Weber rolled the dice. Eleven! Weber picked up the gold piece, kissed it and put it in his vest pocket. Bob Rowe removed the diamond rings from his fingers, the watch from his pocket, the gold garter bands off his socks, his cuff links and he laid them on the table, saying calmly, "That jewelry amounts to nine hundred dollars. You can pawn them for six hundred, take my word."

Weber said, "Mr. Rowe, I believe you."

Weber rolled the dice as the large crowd anxiously looked on in silence and amazement. When the dice stopped rolling, Mr. Rowe smiled, saying, "Kid, the dice says seven."

The large crowd grunted but did not mumble a word. They were in sympathy with Mr. Rowe and would not dare offend or embarrass him. But they marveled at the masterful dice rolling of the youngster. Around the dice table stood many pimps and their women, all dressed in their finest regalia. Mr. Rowe said, smiling, "Kid, you've won all the money. Pick it up, it's all yours."

Cheekey John, who was standing behind Weber, took his Stetson hat and helped Weber to sort and take up the large pile of money. There were all sorts of whispered comments complimenting Weber's dice rolling. Chinee Morris, who was standing there between two of his beautiful quadroon whores and had lost all of his own money said, angrily, "If I just had some more money I'd bet the kid. His luck's gotta change! The law of averages proves that."

Cheekey John heard him and looked up. Weber yelled to the waiter and bartender, "Give everybody in the bar as much as they can drink for as long as they drink."

Chinee Morris said, angrily, "If I just had some more money."

Cheekey John looked at the fingers of the beautiful women and said sarcastically, "Take them rings off your whores' fingers and bet them."

Chinee Morris yelled back, "I'll bet them."

He grabbed the hands of the surprised women, pulled off their rings and threw them on the table. John picked up the five rings and looked at them carefully, saying, "Ladies. How much did these rings cost?"

The women tell him they are valued at five hundred dollars. John laughs and says to Weber, who is smiling at the women, "Shoot Weber! Take this fool's women's rings."

Weber rolls the dice...seven.

Bob Rowe smiles and says, "The dominoes say seven!"

One of the women starts to cry. John says, "Don't cry, li'l girl, we'll give you your rings back, don't cry."

Chinee Morris yells, "Bitch, stop crying! I'll buy a hundred rings, shut up before I kick your ass, you chicken-hearted bitch. I'm quitting your ass anyhow." Then Chinee scowls and says "You know damned well I'm broke."

John says nicely "No you ain't, Chinee. Weber could use one or two of your whores – bet them!"

Everybody looks around at one another, surprised. They had heard of such bets but never seen one. Chinee frowns, looks at the two women and says, "Okay, that's a bet."

John says, "How much value you put on the little ladies?"

Chinee says, "Five hundred apiece."

The two women start crying. Chinee hollers, "Shut up, you two bitches, you are bad luck anyhow!"

John counts one thousand dollars, places them on the table and says, "Come here, little girls, to your new daddies." Then he tells Weber, "Shoot the dice, Weber."

Weber rolls the dice. When the dice stop the crowd yell, "Seven".

John says, "Come to your new daddies, sweethearts."

The women don't move; they just stand there crying like babies. Chinee hollers, "Get away from me, you two bad-luck bitches." The women start screaming and howling but the piano player, Red Cayou, drowns out the noise by pressing down on the loud pedal on the piano and playing extra loud.

Chinee walks off through the crowd to the bar. John walks over to the two women and puts their rings back on their fingers and then wipes their eyes with his handkerchief. While he is comforting the women, he hears, "Gimme ten kid, gimme twenty kid, gimme five kid."

He looks around and sees Weber surrounded by a group of the roughest bullies in the city. John leaves the women and pushes the bullies aside, taking the hat full of money and jewelry from Weber and yelling: "Nobody gets a god-damn cent and if they do, it'll be over my dead body. This morning little Weber ain't giving a living ass one red penny. That means, he ain't giving a cripple crab a crutch! And the first bad sonofabitch that tries to take some of this kid's money I surriligate his ass, and if you don't believe me, just try. I'll go to hell with somebody this morning. If I'm lying, God ain't my secret judge."

The thugs stood back, angrily watching John and little Weber. John says, "And you half-bad sons of bitches can wait for us outside if you doubt my word."

John tells a friend, "Go to the checkroom and get my two forty fives."

The friend rushes off and returns with the two weapons. John places them inside his belt and calls the two women, who are smiling now. He tells the waiter, "Bring me a bottle of the best whisky!" and he sits the owner down. He tells Weber "Sit down," then beckons to Bob Rowe who is smiling and enjoying the scene. The waiter brings the whisky and serves it. John looks at the thugs who are still standing around, mumbling to each other and says, sternly, "Nobody takes nothing from nobody. The only thing that will be given away this morning is hot burning steel blue jackets from those two forty fives."

He calls the waiter and says, "Give those gentlemen a quart of whisky to give them some nerve, 'cause I ain't kidding this morning."

The waiter serves the thugs the whisky which the thugs slowly accept and drink. Then he tells the waiter, "Bring a couple of bottles of whisky to Buddy Petit's band and tell Buddy to play *The Graveyard Blues*."

Then he asks the waiter what the damage is (the bill.) The waiter tells him, he digs into his pocket, pulls out a roll and pays the bill.

Bob Rowe, who is sitting at the table and smiling, says to Weber, "Kid, you're a fine gambler, you are real game and calm, you got a fine future before you. Who taught you how to gamble?"

Weber says, "Nobody. I just love to play and I watch what I'm doing. I practise a lot. I can just about tell how many times the dice roll. I got a special way. I pick them up and roll them and just practise all the time, that's all."

Bob Rowe says, "I got to give it to you, you 'bout the best I've seen. I kept fading you just to see you roll em. You're a master."

Weber said, "Thank you, Mr Rowe."

John looked at the thugs who are now smiling and drinking and said, loud enough for them to hear, "Bob, I wish some sonofabitch would just put a hand on this kid."

Bob Rowe said, "Forget about it, John. They know you ain't joking."

John calls the waiter and says, "Where's Chinee Morris?"

The waiter says, "Chinee has gone; he got a drink at the bar and staggered off. I'll see if I can find him."

Weber says, "Mr. Rowe, I want to give you back your jewelry."

Bob Rowe says, "No, kid. You know, I've got plenty more. Keep it in memory of tonight. You won it all fair and square. It's mighty nice of you. You're a real sport. I'm proud of you. I mean it. It's too bad you're so young. I'd set you up, but them police are real rough on minors. I'll see, maybe I can straighten things in the

District for you. You got a great future. How old are you, kid?"

Weber says, "I'll be eighteen next month."

"Where do you live?"

Weber says, "I stay in the Battlefield, on Perdido near Bolivar."

"Are you married, kid?"

Weber says, "No sir, I live with my Maw."

"That's nice. You're single. What you gonna do with these women you won from Chinee Morris?"

Weber looked at the women without smiling and said, "I don't know, maybe they don't want me; maybe they still loves Chinee."

One of the women says, "No, I'll never go back to Chinee after the way he acted tonight in front of all these people."

Bob Rowe says, "Well, that's up to you. The kid here's got iron nerves and he's a coming boy, young and good looking. Both of you all look like white. It's no telling how far you all can go. You can leave this town and go away and pass for white. You're both young and smart. This town is going to the dogs. It's getting worser and worser. What's your name, li'l girl?"

The woman says, "My name is Christine Bijou."

"Where you work?"

"I work at Lulu White's," the girl says, "and I know you, Mr. Rowe, Lulu talks about you all the time."

Bob raises his eyebrows, surprised. "She says you are the only colored man she could go for, that is, give her money to."

Bob Rowe says, "That's nice. But does she know Chinee is your man?"

Christine says, "No. If she did, she'd fire me, 'cause she don't allow her girls to have colored men. She can't find out 'cause she don't come round colored places or people."

John, who is talking very seriously to the other woman, stops to listen as Buddy Petit begins to play *Home Sweet Home*.

He pours a drink for the party. They drink and he calls a toast. Bob Rowe says to Weber and Christine, "Kids, if you two can get an understanding, you can't help but have success. Weber, come around Twenty Five and see me and take this girl home and make her happy."

Weber says, "Chinee might start some trouble."

John says, nastily, "Don't you worry 'bout Chinee. I'll handle him if he bothers you."

Weber, John and the two women leave. Weber asks John, "Where we going?"

John laughs and says, "Whitefolks, we are going somewhere where it is real quiet and the beds are soft and fluffy."

* * *

In the meantime, Mr. Rowe chartered two cattle cars on the Southern Pacific Railroad, a couple of days before he departed and absconded with the Helping Hand Society's treasure. He loaded one of the two cattle cars (which the railroad company had conveniently left in a siding, at his request,) with most of the household furnishings from his woman Ready Money's brothel, which bore the well known name "The Garden of Eaten."

The famous garden was reputed to be one of the District's most beautiful meat markets and that included the flesh pots of Lulu White and Bucktown Bessie. Mr. Rowe loaded the six beautiful, expensive, highly polished master brass beds, all his dozens of box-back suits and most of Read Money's clothing. He packed all the silk and satin bed clothes and also the brass spitoons and slop jars. Mr. Rowe's provisions for his companion and himself were carefully cooked and prepared by Cookshop's cook. The victuals for the long journey consisted of:

    2 clothes baskets full of fried chicken
    1 washtub full of cat heads (biscuits)
    2 hampers full of boiled shrimp
    2 hampers of stuffed crabs
    2 boiled hams
    2 stuffed turkeys
    100 pork chops (breaded)

When Ready Money's neighbors asked if she was moving, she was ready with her explanation. She said she was getting rid of the old furniture and buying new furniture because after she straightened out those dirty police, business would be better than ever in the District for everybody. Bob Rowe even loaded the piano on the cattle car. When Ready Money laid off her girls she did so with the excuse that the police had heard about her plans to fight them and the girls should hide out until after the big ball was over. Then she'd give them the signal that all was calm, and they could start making a peaceful and decent living again. So the girls scattered to all parts of the city.

Everbody in the District bought tickets to the big ball for the Helping Hand Society. Ready Money personally made the rounds of all the business places in the District, from the highest to the lowest, selling tickets.

The night of the ball everyone showed up and hundreds of people were turned away. Joe Oliver's band played for the affair which lasted until after four in the morning. There was not much dancing because the hall was packed to overflowing; the guests just stood about the hall laughing, talking and drinking toasts to the good days ahead which Ready Money had prophesied.

After the ball was over, Ready Money gathered up all of the money from the bar, kitchen, hat check room and the box office. She stood at the door of the hall and assured the crowd as they left for home that she was having a meeting with the city officials later in the morning and that they would meet her at Big Twenty Five the next night when she would give them the good news that the police were to leave the people of the District alone.

After the crowd left, Ready Money hurried home to her man, Mr. Bob Rowe. They sat at the dining room table and counted the receipts of the ball and the hundreds of tickets that had been sold in advance. The money amounted to forty-five hundred dollars. Mr. Rowe placed the bills in a money belt which he wore around his waist and the silver into a valise. He kissed Ready Money and went out to the Southern Pacific freight yard. Awaiting him there was the smiling Mr. Barrel of Fun and inside one of the cattle cars under a pile of green alfalfa hay hid six of Mr. Rowe's cronies who would ride to California free, which was against the rules, the law, and the contract Mr. Rowe had signed with the railroad company. The six cronies were carefully schooled by Mr. Barrel of Fun to be as quiet as mice until the train was well on its way; then he would signal them to come out from under the hay for air and food. They were to hide under the hay at every stop on the way to California because if a brakeman or switchman or yard detective saw them it meant jail and trouble. They followed his instructions perfectly. When the train stopped they hid and when it rolled, they came out, sat on the hay and gambled all the way to California. The carefully picked friends of Mr. Rowe were Chinee Morris, Jimmy the Fixer, Eddie Lindsay, Flim Flam Sam Depass, Cheekey John and Whitefolks Weber.

The engineer on the freight train looked out of the window of the cabin on the large steam engine, then at his watch. When the minute hand ticked off seven a.m., he pulled the throttle, the fireman rang the bell, blew the whistle and the train slowly rolled on its cross country journey. When the freight sped through the first little town, Barrel of Fun yelled and kidded the boys, saying "Boys, we're going to heaven, come up for air!"

No sooner had the boys emerged from under the haystack than Whitefolks came up with two decks of cards and cleared a spot. He started ruffling the cards while the other men picked the hay from their clothes. As the train rolled West, Bob Rowe and Barrel of Fun sat at their end talking about their future plans with the horses. Whitefolks and the boys gambled, played cotch and poker. They laughed about how their deserted women would act and feel when they realized they had left New Orleans, and left the women flat.

They laughed, joked, ate and gambled as the fast freight rolled West.

* * *

There was very little said as Ready Money sat at the large table in her brothel, watching Bob Rowe sort and count the profits from the ball given by the Helping Hand Society. She smiled an inner satisfaction, having performed her part of the plan to leave New Orleans. She was thrilled and happy because she saw that Bob

Rowe was happy as he counted the money. Once again she had proven to Bob that she was his woman and his only, and that as long as she had breath in her body she was his "ace in the hole." Bob and she had been through thick and thin. She was his woman and he was her man. They were like two peas in a pod; had a perfect understanding; never quarreled and rarely disagreed. They had vowed to be true to each other and true they were.

When they decided to leave New Orleans, that was that. If that would make him happy, it would make her happy because the happiness she received out of life was in just living to make her man happy.

They had met and started when young in life and never once did either become boring to the other. For the past ten years they had prospered together and could look back at few failures and regrets. Bob was number one man in the District and she was number one women. When Bob buckled the money belt around his waist, and took the satchel full of silver money, he kissed her fondly. He said but a few words and they were very tender words: "Darling, I love you. Keep acting the part like I told you. See you in California in three weeks. So long, baby!"

When Bob Rowe walked out of the brothel, Ready Money watched him as he walked away and down the street. She didn't cry because she knew that in three weeks she would be with him once again.

When Bob had disappeared out of sight she closed her door, went into the kitchen, opened a bottle of whisky and poured herself a big drink. Then she went to the bathroom and turned on the water for a hot bath. She undressed, took a bath and set her clock for four o'clock in the afternoon. She took another long drink and went to bed.

Four o'clock. The clock rang. She got up and went to the front door. She called a kid who was playing in the street, gave him ten cents and told him to go to the fruit stand and buy her ten cents worth of red onion. When the child came back with the onions she went to the kitchen, cut a half dozen onions in half, put the rest in handkerchiefs and placed them in handy seclusion all about the house. She fixed herself some lunch, drank some more whisky, sat at the table and thought about Bob Rowe, trying to picture him on the train, with his horses and Barrel of Fun.

At seven o'clock, when the District began to stir and come to life, she took a coffee can full of nickels and went to the phone, opened the phone book and started to call everybody and every place in the District she knew. Her prepared speech on the phone went like this, (it was very secretive and confidential.)

"Hello. This is Ready Money, Bob Rowe's wife. Have you seen Bob? Well, this morning before ten o'clock he left home with seven thousand dollars. There was forty five hundred dollars of the money from the Helping Hand Society's Ball and twenty five hundred dollars of his and my money. He had an appointment with the Mayor and the District Attorney. He went to pay them the money so they would stop those rotten police and detectives from interfering with our business establishments here in the District.

"I don't know what happened to him, but will you spread the word around that I haven't seen him since this morning at around nine-thirty when he left here with the seven thousand dollars? Do me a favor and spread the news around. If anybody saw him after ten o'clock, please call me. Maybe he was held up and robbed. If you hear or see anything of him please call me. My number is Central 8808. Thank you very kindly; I'm so worried I don't know what to do."

Ready Money whispered the story to Pete Lala, Joe Lala, Spano, at Big Twenty Five, the Boudoir. By nine o'clock that night the news had spread like an evening tide; everybody talking, gossiping, expressing all sorts of clues and opinions.

The members who had joined the Helping Hand Society weren't too concerned about the money they had paid as membership fees, because money was plentiful in the District and the twenty dollars they had paid to join was a pittance. They were mostly concerned about the whereabouts of Bob Rowe and upset by his mysterious disappearance. He was very well liked and respected and most of the gossip was in sympathy for his welfare and safety.

The rumors spread:

Maybe he was in jail.
Maybe he had been robbed.
Maybe he was kidnapped.
Maybe he was killed by gunmen.
Maybe the police had pulled in him.
Maybe he was in the hospital.
Maybe he had been threatened and was in hiding.

At twelve o'clock that night Ready Money's brothel was packed and jammed by the District's big shots. They ordered and drank whisky and consoled Ready Money who was crying hysterically, lying on a bed and on the verge of collapse.

Her friends sent out searching parties. They called the hospitals, the morgue, all the jails and precincts, all the tonks, cabarets, dives, sporting houses, all Bob Rowe's known friends. That went on all night. They contacted Tom Anderson and Pete Lala, who had an in with the police department, to find out if the police were holding Bob secretly. Next day, as the mourning at Ready Money's house continued, a cook on the railroad came by and after a few drinks he told the gathering that he would kiss a Bible and swear that he saw Bob Rowe and Barrel of Fun standing in a cattle car, looking at the siding of a freight train that was bound for California. He said that he had stepped to the window of the diner on the train he was on for some air because it was very hot in the kitchen. He looked out the window and saw Bob Rowe and Barrel of Fun. Fun saw him and ducked but he did get a good look at Bob Rowe and he wondered at the time what they were doing on that freight train. He also said that he thought he had seen horses. He kept talking as the crowd looked and listened. Then he suggested that Ready Money call up the Southern Pacific Railroad and try to learn where they had gone.

When Ready Money heard that she gave out a scream and fainted. The cook called the railroad and as the crowd listened he repeated what was told him on the phone: "Yes! Yes! Yes! You say Mr. Rowe is traveling with six horses on freight train no. 117? Destination San Diego, California? Thank you, thank you very much, mister, for your kindness. Yes, thank you a million."

He hung up the receiver, saying, "I told you all I saw Bob and Fun on that train. My eyes don't fool me. You can bet your ass if I say I saw 'em I saw 'em."

Those in the crowd looked at one another, waiting for a word or comment, but not a word was said. One of the women went to the bathroom, took a douche bag from the wall, then she went to the ice box in the kitchen and filled the bag with ice. She came back into the bedroom and put the douche bag on Ready Money's head while everyone looked on. In a few moments Ready Money moved and opened her eyes. She said,"What happened?"

The woman who held the douche bag to her head said, "Money, when we called up the railroad station and you heard the news that Bob had gone to California, the shock was too much for you. You went out like a light."

Ready Money asked,"Is that a fact that Bob has left me? I can't believe it. That's a rotten dirty trick to pull on me. Good as I was to that man, I just can't believe it, I just can't. If he didn't want me he could have told me. It would have been all right. I should have known it; he's been telling me we was tired of New Orleans. Yes. Him and Barrel of Fun. They took them horses and have gone to California."

Ready Money sat up on the side of her bed. She shook her head as if to clear it; she reached under the pillow and pulled out her pocketbook which she opened and emptied on the bed. She looked at the contents: a powder puff, hairpins, keys, powder box, perfume bottle, a rabbit's foot, comb, rouge, two one-dollar bills, and sixty cents in change. She spread the coins out with her finger and counted them slowly. She shook her head sadly and said, "Nice as I've been to Bob, he goes and leaves me with two dollars and sixty cents. Just to think he cares more for the goddamned horses than he does for me."

One of the women poured her a large drink of whisky; Ready Money drank it down, then she gritted her teeth and frowned and tightened her fists.

She swore:"So help me, God, if Bob has run out on me, I swear on my dead Mother's head, I'll find him and kill him or my name ain't Ready Money. He took that money, saying he was going to the officials and pay them off so we could have some peace in the District. How am I gonna face my friends? Over four thousand dollars of their money gone and he left me to face the music. How can I face you all after you all putting your trust in me? I'll kill that no-good rotten bastard. I'll find him and that two faced Barrel of Fun. That sonofabitch is the one who inveigled Bob to leave here with him and them goddamned horses. I gave Bob the best portion of my life. I was more than a mother to him. I hustled, robbed, begged and did everything under the sun to make him happy and that consumptive bastard ran out on me, and left me holding the bag.

"All the money he left me in this world to my name is two dollars and sixty cents. I couldn't treat a dog like that! Oh, but he'll pay. Where's my furniture? He said he was going to sell it to the second hand man and buy new furniture. Oh that sneaking, no good sonofabitch. Just look at me: the great Ready Money with just two dollars and sixty cents to her name. I just can't believe it."

The cook dug into his pocket and came up with a roll of money and said, "Here's some money, Ready," giving her twenty dollars. "This will help you along."

Ready Money bowed her head and said, "Thank you, I'll give it back to you."

Everyone in the crowd began to give her money, the men peeling off their rolls and the women going into their bosoms and stockings. Ready Money said, "Thanks. This is towards my fare to California. As soon as I get railroad fare and enough money to pay a lawyer to bail me out of jail, I'll head straight for San Diego, wherever that is, in California and kill Bob's no good ass! If I don't, my name ain't Ready Money."

She took a chair, went to the armoire, stood up on the chair, reached on top of the armoire and got a blue steel forty-five pistol. "This is the first time in my life I've ever thought of killing anybody, but I'm gonna kill Bob Rowe. I'm gonna empty this gun in his guts."

She poured herself a long drink of whisky and wiped her eyes with a handkerchief from the mantelpiece. (She had squeezed the onion inside of the handkerchief and the tears flowed as the

The exterior of 1027 Chartres Street in the French Quarter of New Orleans. The left-hand house is 1027, and a plaque on the front wall commemorates Danny Barker's birth there in 1909. (Alyn Shipton)

Inset: Danny's daughter, Sylvia, in front of the room in the former slave quarters behind 1027 Chartres where Danny was born. (Alyn Shipton)

The Pythian Roof Garden Orchestra in 1925, a band containing Bolden's one-time bassist Jimmy Johnson. Other personnel (whose names are added in Danny's script on the print) are Alfred Williams, drums; Earl Humphrey, trombone; Osceola Blanchard, piano; Eddie Cherie, tenor sax; Manuel Perez, leader and cornet; Adolphe Alexander, alto sax; Maurice Durand, cornet; Caffery Danensburg, banjo. The venue was operated by Willie Washington five nights a week until the venue became part of the Charity Hospital. (Danny Barker Collection)

Right: Chick Leg, or One Leg Horace, King of the Second Liners, pictured shortly before he retired from parading in 1960. (Danny Barker Collection)

One Leg Horace surrounded by an all-star brass band in 1960. Personnel include (left to right) Kid Thomas, trumpet; Booker T. Glass, snare drum; Manuel Paul, tenor sax; Horace; Kid Shiek, trumpet; Ernie Cagnoletti, trumpet; Albert Warner (obscured), trombone; Noon Johnson, trombone; Harold Dejan, alto sax; Eddie Summers, trombone; unknown, sousaphone. (Danny Barker Collection)

Hamp Benson, 1946.
(Danny Barker Collection)

306 - N. 15ᵗʰ Place
Springfield, Illinois
June 17, 1946

Jazzland Research Guild
1185 Fulton Ave.
Bronx, N.Y.C.

Mr. Danny Barker :-
Instead of filling out your questionnaire, I
find it is easier for me to write it in my
own words.
This is just a sketch & the beginning of my
musical life. I could go further into details
if it is necessary & helpful. I haven't given
you any of the time when I was on top & in
"big time" as I am planning on writing a book myself.
I thanks for giving me the chance of
appearing in your book.
Enclosed is your photo of me. Thanks again.
Sincerely-
Hamp Benson.

First page of Hamp Benson's
letter to Danny, the rest of
which is reproduced in
Chapter 5.

Blue Lu and Danny Barker at home in New York at the time of the Jazzland Research Guild.
(Blue Lu Barker Collection: photo by Martin Lichtner)

JAZZLAND RESEARCH GUILD

Questionnaire for Musicians and Performers

1. Date _May 23rd 1946_

2. Full name (including nickname) _Adolphe L. Alexander (T#TS)_

3. Date of birth _15th_ _July_ _1898 -_
   Day   Month   Year

4. Place of birth _New Orleans La._

5. What instrument do you play? (including doubles) If reed, indicate exactly. Mark specialty with an X _Alto Sax + Clarinet B Flat Baritone_

6. If not an instrumentalist, mark with an X which of the following is your profession: performer____, singer____, dancer____, concert artist____, comedian____, promoter____

7. In what city did you attend high school? _New Orleans_ College? _None_

8. Did you study your profession at school? Privately? On your own? With special teachers? _Apprentis teacher Prof. Gholiquy + Prof. Louis Gier_

9. When did you begin your professional education and activities? Give a brief outline of these activities, and how long they continued.
   I began playing Clarinet in 1920 after studying for 2 year's in 1916 I started the Trumpet for about 2 years I gave up the Trumpet for the Clarinet in 1921 I began playing Alto Sax and the B.F. Clarinet in Nov 1935 I began playing the Saxophone my baritone used to play

---

22. Who is, or was your favorite jazz star, instrumentalist, or singer? (this pertains to all fields)
    Lorenzo Tio, Clarinet & John Lindsee Guitaris

23. Write a few humorous incidents in your travels. You may write as much as you desire, using additional paper, if this space is not sufficient.
    While playing with the ship Capt. on Steam Island Juliene 1926 on a moonlight ride in Hickmore Ky. A. Hill Billy Rebel I walked to play Michelius very after we had already played it. Sidney Leblanc we had another report he called the Capt. lark. Mark Frob from his Clipper And arrived & around me his finger and cord spread oregan Letter playin I said now Sidney sent the pistol and immediately began playing the Mr. sent me overside of Vicksburg 1920

24. If you play more than one instrument, please list. _Clarinet, E flat Bf Baritone_

25. What is your home address? _2421 St. Anthony, New Orleans, La._
    St.   City   State

26. What is your mailing address, from which letters can be forwarded to you?
    At Present Company 112 B. 97th Av. 99 N. Y. - Original
    Address 2421 St. Anthony at New Orleans La.

10. Exactly when did you launch your professional career? What show, group or band and circumstances? _1920 with Kid Rena? with Kimball? Brass Band_

11. Where did you work? With whom? _In N.O. & also with the Ork. Maretin Gene_

12. With what other shows, night clubs, cabarets, or bands have you been with since then? List in chronological order and give approximate length of time with each. XX those with which you recorded.
Piron Ork. at Gook chere Night Club two mo.
Sidney Ork. Little Club six mo.
Eddie Jackson orpheum Ork. Astoby come Hall three mo.
Willie Pajeaud Ork. Clena Gity Dance Hall 2 mo.
Deslimes Ork. Tranclime Night Blut 2 mt.
... in 1924 Sidney's Desvigne Ork. 1927 Desvigne Ork.
1928 1929 1930 till 1932 went in the Navy Band
1922 Trombone Quartet 1923 manager Ruben and

13. If soloist, on specifically what records or show of any kind, have you taken solos? Give as complete a list as possible, naming band or show and title
English Elma of the Deslimes of Atlanta first of Rythm Marrey Band
from me Again Pr. P.A. Band Dom home Jaz tuylath Ork High Brid
Sidney's Desvigne Band

14. Have you played or engaged in radio programs, either in commercial or sustaining? Give details. _Broadcast with the Parisine rorg Harlem one Cor. L._
one night a week. And at Antrach with Sidney Ork. mo 10.1917
And with the French Ork at Pensacola Fla. & Creefort Miss

15. Have you composed or arranged? Give details. _____

16. List your ancestors and relatives in the jazz field, or any other field in which you are engaged
My Uncle Willie Ply or the Cornet played played
Ragtime music in the old days my Daddy played
cornet. the old days dad played alto horn & Bb Baritones
_my father Cha... __ brother played Cornet Clifford Jazz_
played Jazz and Bb bass Clivel Gold took class in the respatin place

18. What is most important in your field that is worth being known by more people? _____
playing for different & Benifits

19. List your likes and dislikes about the field in which you are engaged
I like to travel place to place meeting different people
I dislike standing in one position one job very tired

20. What Band or performer was, or is tops, during your stay in New Orleans?
Robert Turefields Ork. And Sidney Desvigne Ork.

21. Pick your All Time, All Star Jazz Band; Seven who you would like to hear again.

Cornet. _Buddy Petite_

Trombone _Manuel Frenchy_

Clarinet _Lorenzo Tio_

Guitar or Banjo. _Johnny Dingler_

String Bass. _Jimmy Johnson_

Drums. _Kid Hoggett_

Piano. _Camilla Gold_

Danny in a Cab Calloway Orchestra publicity shot, taken during the period covered in Chapter 6. (Cab Calloway Collection, Boston)

onion juice burned her eyes.)

She asked the cook, "Where is San Diego? How long will it take me to get there? How much will the fare cost?"

She looked at the two diamond rings on her fingers and said, "I'll pawn these rings and get ready to go and fix up Mr. Bob Rowe, the son of a bitch. Let's get some more whisky."

The cook provided the money and sent someone out for the whisky.

Ready Money then spoke of her past with Bob Rowe as everyone listened. She said, "I been with Bob fifteen years. The first night I met him, he put me to work in Patty Lee's house and the first week with him I gave him four hundred dollars: the money from selling my body to them nasty Paddies. In those fifteen years there wasn't one day that passed that I did not keep him happy with more money than any pimp in the District. All those years I lived just for Bob Rowe. I bought him diamonds, horses, clothes. He could always call me or send to get money if he was gambling. That's how I got the name Ready Money, 'cause I never let him down. And this is how he thanks me, skipping town and showing me his ass!"

Then Ready Money turned to one of the girls nearby, a little pretty child, a young whore who was her little pet, to whom she was teaching the serious business of whoring. She said to her, "Go down to the hardware store, and get me a box of steel jacket bullets." And she shouted loudly again, for all the folks in her big house to hear: "I'm goin' to California and kill that no good sonofabitch. I'm gonna light his ass up like a Christmas tree, so help me, God, and if Barrel of Fun is there when I find Bob, his black ass goes too, so Bob'll have some company down below. And that is where he's going. Down in Hell!"

"Somebody –please give me a drink."

One of the women says, "Easy, you better eat something. All that whisky ain't no good."

Ready Money says, "I can't eat, I can't eat. There's just one thing on my mind and that's to find and kill Bob Rowe and that rotten Barrel of Fun."

She got back into bed and talked on and on about how she

was a slave for Bob and how she would kill him. For four days Ready did not leave the house. She did not dress. She only wore a slip and *crêpe-de-chine* robe. She did not comb her hair or powder and rouge her face. The continued use of the onion-soaked handkerchiefs caused her eyes to stay red and puffed. During the four days, everybody of importance visited her and listened to her ravings and they offered condolences and gave her money. She was assured by more than a few of the District big shots that after she had killed Bob, all she had to tell the judge was that Bob forced her into a life of sin and that he had lived off her earnings as a prostitute, and then the judge would turn her loose.

It was like the time that Clerk Wade was slain (and so many other pimps). Her brothel stayed crowded with people coming and going. She went to the bathroom and counted the money in her pocket book. It amounted to seven hundred dollars. The cook, who had become a constant visitor, sat there at her bedside and before all the folks, while he ogled her half naked body, he made plans for her ticket and transportation. He sympathetically told her about the trip to California: where she could hide until she located Bob and Fun and how she could kill them both during the night and come back to New Orleans; that she could always depend on him to look out for her because he liked her as a friend and that a friend in need is a friend indeed. She looked right into his eyes and listened between sobs and thanked him for his kindness. He also told her how, at the trial after the killing, he would go to California to testify on her behalf, because he felt so sorry for her.

Reverend Sunshine heard the hundreds of stories and all the gossip and came by to see Ready Money. He listened to her sad tales of woe and he begged her to reconsider all her plans of murder and revenge. She told him it was no use, because Bob Rowe had done her wrong and they both were bound for Hell. Reverend Sunshine gave her some money and departed.

Ready sent Rotten Rosie to Maison Blanche, a big department store, to get a black outfit to travel in. She told Rosie that she knew that after she had killed Bob she would have to serve some time in the penitentiary (maybe two to five years) so she was going to give Rosie the brothel and the furniture that was still there.

Rotten Rosie was respected as one of the District's most daring and ruthless sporting women. The name, Rotten Rosie, was given to her when the gossip spread that she had forced her fourteen-year-old daughter into prostitution. As the story went, she noticed that her young daughter's breasts were getting extra large and also that her backside was bouncing about rather loosely. She had tried her best to raise the girl decently, in spite of the fact that they lived in the District amongst all sorts of vice, sin and temptation. Everybody respected the girl, who was called Little Rosebud. As was her custom, when twilight descended on the District, Rose would leave Little Rosebud in the three-room house along, while she went to her crib to hustle. One of the neighbors told her that a young man of the neighborhood would visit Little Rosebud after Rosie left. So Rosie doubled back one night and found Rosebud and the youngster in bed, moaning soulfully of their love for one another. When Rosie tiptoed into the house she listened, grabbed an iron frying pan, then sneaked into the bedroom and whipped the lovers all about the place. She chased the young man into the street although he had no pants on. The young man running from the house – pantsless – caused little excitement because this was a common sight.

Rose was not concerned about hiding her daughter's disgrace or of forcing the young man to marry Rosebud. He had the reputation of being a trifler and he was considered simple. She whipped Little Rosebud unmercifully, damned near killing her. A couple of days after the black and blue bruises had disappeared, She gave her daughter the following lecture:

"You rotten, stinking, little no-good bitch!I've been trying to raise you decent and respectable and all the time you are giving away your body free and for nothing. Since you are a woman now and big enough to lay down under a man you are going to get your ass out of here and hustle – just like me – and get paid for it."

So she painted Little Rosebud's face with powder, rouge and lipstick and they hustled tricks side by side. It was a scandal for a while but as something new and spectacular was happening daily, the comments were, "So what!"

The cook and a dozen of her friends went to the railroad station with Ready Money. The cook bought her ticket, took her to her seat on the train and the friends all kissed her goodbye and wished her *bon voyage*.

As the train pulled out of the station slowly, she looked out of the window of the train and threw kisses to the cook, who was waving to her and crying. When she rolled away and was out of sight she frowned and said, "You no good bastard."

She relaxed in her seat and then smiled saying, "Four days and I'll meet my Bob."

* * *

When the fast Southern Pacific freight train slowed down and rolled into the freight yards of the station at San Diego, California, Mr. Barrel of Fun stopped the card game that had been in progress since the train had left New Orleans. He told the boys to crawl back under the hay and stay there until he gave them the signal to come out. When the train came to a stop he opened the door, and stepped down, followed by Bob Rowe. The railroad yard dispatcher came up and told them where the two cattle cars would be placed by the switch engine.

Bob Rowe just looked on, as all this was new to him. Barrel of Fun signed the papers and gave them back to the dispatcher as he had done many times before, traveling with the Greentree Stables. It was five o'clock in the afternoon. He and Bob Rowe went to a phone and he called the company that hauled horses from the railroad to the racetrack. Then he leased a stable at the racetrack for the season. At nine o'clock that night, under the cover of darkness, three large vans arrived at the siding and the horses and furniture were loaded on the vans quickly and quietly and taken to the racetrack. As soon as Bob Rowe and Barrel of Fun arrived at the track, they went to the office and paid three months' rent in advance for the stable for the horses.

The stable was the oldest and most dilapidated structure on the track. Barrel of Fun and the smart boys from New Orleans unloaded the horses and led them inside the stalls. They fed the horses and watered them. While doing so they looked in a corner and found an old Mexican lying there, asleep and snoring. They didn't awaken him; they let him sleep. After unloading the furniture and the piano, the boys washed up, put on their best clothes and went on the town. Barrel of Fun stayed at the stable and watched the horses.

The next morning when the boys came back to the stable they saw Barrel of Fun and the old Mexican sitting at a table, eating a breakfast of ham and eggs and laughing and talking like old friends. He introduced the old Mexican to the boys, saying "This is Miguel, he is trainer of horses from old Mexico. He knows a whole lot about horses; things I've never heard before. He's broke and busted because they won't give him a trainer's license. He has no money and nowhere to stay, that's why he is sleeping in this stable. So, fellows, treat him nice 'cause he can help me train these horses."

Bob Rowe and the boys all said okay. The old Mexican, Barrel of Fun and Bob Rowe went from stable to stable, examining the six horses. The Mexican looked at their hooves, legs, nostrils, eyes, and teeth and said, "Me show you nice fellows how to make horse run faster than the birds, the wind, the storm: like lightning!"

Bob Rowe said, "That's what I would like to see."

Miguel said, "Let horses rest for few days, then start the exercise."

Bob says okay and tells Barrel of Fun, "I'm renting a large rooming house for the boys to stay. We'll have to rough it until Ready Money arrives and fixes it up."

Cheekey John says, "I'm buying some pots and pans to cook 'cause I don't like the way these people in town mess up that food." Bob Rowe and the boys go back to town.

Three days later Miguel hires a small skinny Mexican youth to exercise and ride the horses. Each morning the six horses gallop around the track and are clocked.

Two of the horses were entered in races and both of them came in first. The speed of the horses had improved greatly: the light, fresh, cool air and sunshine combined with the benefit of a special diet that old Miguel prepared and fed the horses before each race were responsible. This diet consisted of a generous portion of Loco Weed (better known as marijuana,) a pint measure of Mexican Jumping Beans, one dozen pimento peppers. This was mixed with the oats and hay. Two hours before post time the horse was given water to drink and this water was spiked with a quart of one hundred and ten proof tequila.

The horses became a sensation on the track. They rarely ran out of the money and Mr. Bob Rowe won a fortune. Five years later, when he died of T.B., he was very wealthy and owned lots of real estate.

3
Creole Songs

I have heard many tales and theories that jazz music came from slaves on the Southern plantations, but when I was a small boy in the Creole section of New Orleans, I heard folks singing whole songs from top to bottom in French and Patois, just like you hear Bing Crosby singing *Blue Skies* or *I Got Rhythm*. These songs were full of spirit and had a beat, and on Mardi Gras Day, you would hear groups of maskers singing in Creole Patois and dancing the Bombouche (Bom-bu-shay.) The West Indian islanders do the same dance at their social affairs in New York City. I heard these songs all over the neighborhood. Catholic Creole women doing house work and nursing their babies sing these songs and not the Protestant hymns and spirituals. I used to wonder about these colored people singing French songs. Most of these songs seemed to ridicule someone and if you listed intently you could bet you'd hear the phrase "moi chere".

The first school I attended was a private school supervised by Mr. Nelson Medard and it was called Medard School. In New Orleans he was considered and respected as a very brilliant gentleman. The school was located at his home. He and his two daughters taught the children and his two sons worked for the Federal Government and were reputed to have high positions with the diplomatic service.

About a hundred and fifty students attended the school and we all sat in one big room, on wooden benches at long tables. Mr. Medard sat below a high window on a high desk like in a courtroom and he ruled and taught with iron discipline. Classes started at nine o'clock and closed at three. Recess was from twelve to one but with no wild games and noises that you hear at other schools. No one spoke once class started. When you arrived in the morning and said, "Good morning, Mr. Medard," until you left in the evening and said, "Good day, Mr. Medard," no one spoke a word.

Mr. Medard spoke quite a few languages and a dozen or so foreign kids attended his school. When he used the rattan on them it was funny to hear them bawling in their native language. He taught out of McGuffery books. The tuition was one dollar a month, fifty cents extra for French or Spanish and also fifty cents for music lessons, on piano or violin. His wife and daughters cooked and served hot meals which cost five cents, one nickel: red beans and rice, all kinds of beans, stews and vegetables, and after you drank two glasses of water and brought your plate to the kitchen and washed it, you could buy shelled peanuts and home-made cake and candy. The food was great because he and his family were served out of the same pots. Whenever he scolded a child he would say: "And now go and tell your parents and if they don't like what I gave you I will give them some of the same medicine."

I never saw a parent come to complain and when one would come to visit they were always very polite and respectful. I could always tell when it was near twelve o'clock because he would take a bottle out of his desk and pour out a yellow liquid in a small glass and slowly drink it down. In later years I asked his grandson what was in that bottle and he said it was pure Italian olive oil. During the day he would have visitors, people of all nationalities. They would come and sit and watch the proceedings, whisper questions to him and praise him. When he had visitors you could hear nothing except occasionally a sneeze. But one day five little East Indians, dressed in their turbans and native dress, all colors with long black plaited whiskers, visited us. They had soft sandals on and the class, their heads buried in their books, did not see them enter and bow to Mr. Medard but suddenly somebody giggled, which meant trouble, and when the class saw these strange people everybody started giggling. Mr. Medard was furious but the Indians started laughing also. Then the Professor joined in the laughter 'til everyone was hysterical. Finally, after everyone had calmed down, Mr. Medard said, "Who laughed first?" and the guilty pupil held up his hand and was told to go and get the rattan.

The Professor said to the Indians, "Gentlemen, I am going to show you something you may never have seen before!" He put that pupil's head between his legs and gave him about twenty strokes with the rattan and made him apologize to the Indians, who seemed very upset. With each stroke of the rattan their eyes would pop open as they clenched their fists with fear. He escorted the Indians into his parlor and stayed there until three o'clock. Then he came back to the classroom and sat silently until six o'clock when he started to dismiss the pupils one at a time.

When you attended Medard's school that was something special. Parents boasted that their children went there because you received special training but a lot of people thought his methods were too severe. My relatives gave my mother hell for sending me there and I was taken out and sent to a public school called Marigny School, which was considered the roughest in the city and was located back of the tracks. It was rough but developed the best athletes in town, girls and boys, and as long as I went there the baseball, basketball, volleyball and track teams won the championships every time. Whenever we visited another school for a contest there was always a gang war on our way home.

Mr. Medard was an interpreter for the United States Government and a lot of important people would come to his home and sit out under a tree in his yard with brief cases full of papers and seriously listen to him as he read these papers to them. It was always "Mr. Medard Sir," and I have never seen anyone smoke and enjoy a cigar like he did.

In fact, in all my barnstorming, just one place, and that was Newport, Rhode Island, playing for Mr. Goelet, Stotesbury and a group of millionaires, while watching them relaxing on the patio, talking softly, drinking and smoking, brought back memories of Mr. Medard. Mr. Medard's grandson, who is now the head waiter in Pat O'Brien's famous night club in New Orleans, told me that during slavery a very rich man bought Mr. Medard and, noticing that he was a bright lad and eager for learning, took him to Europe, where he sent him to the best schools and enrolled him in Rome to study for the priesthood. He did not become a priest but did a lot of traveling. Then he came to New Orleans and opened a private school during the Reconstruction. He kept this fact quiet as it was very dangerous to educate Negroes right after the Civil War. His first students were of all races and included children of well-to-do parents, so therefore he wasn't molested. Also, he was known and visited by many professors and educators in New Orleans and vicinity and had private classes at night for white college students.

During recess one day I walked past the tree in his yard and heard him say, "The people in this city do not speak the real French language, it is a bastard tongue they speak."

A few years back, Albert Nicholas recorded four Creole songs for Circle Records. James P. Johnson, who played piano on the date, after hearing my accompaniment to Nick's clarinet solo, joined in with me perfectly and, laughing, said, "You cats from New Orleans ain't nothing but a bunch of West Indians."

We all laughed. Pops Foster who was drinking from a water glass of whisky started joking about his ancestors who came from France and the heart of Africa, but when we noticed Nick was becoming annoyed with the comedy we stopped kidding and became serious. On the four songs Nick sang the vocals and I answered him on a couple and I think my flat southern brogue ruined the records. James P. Johnson fell in perfectly as he was a great musician and it is tragic that the big record companies ignored his talent and only let him record a few of his compositions in his later years. Among the great pianists in America, until Earl Hines and Art Tatum appeared, he was the master, the king, and at the Rhythm Club in New York City he was acknowledged as the boss. He wrote a couple of symphonies but nothing ever happened with them.

He knew so much about music and I asked him many questions. Paddy Harmon, who owned Paddy Harmon's Dreamland, where King Oliver played, copyrighted the homemade mutes that Oliver played and made a fortune selling the popular Harmon mutes. I had heard these were the first mutes used by jazz orchestras, but James P. said European symphony orchestras used a similar small metal mute a couple of hundred years back. Whenever I'd mention Jelly Roll Morton he would always laugh and speak well of Jelly. I'm being carried away about James P., now I'm going back to the Creole records and Pops Foster.

Before we recorded the last song we took a fifteen minute

break and me and Pops Foster started drinking the whisky while James P. played some primitive rhythms on the piano. He said years ago he stayed around Charleston, South Carolina, for a few weeks and he heard music similar to the Creole songs. He started imitating how the natives (the Geechies) spoke. There were some record collectors in the studio and I noticed they were listening in earnest, also that Pops Foster was feeling real good. Teasing Nick, I said, "Pops, tell them about that big snake they caught in New Orleans that time."

Nick looked at me and shook his head disgustedly as if saying to himself, "Now, I've got to hear this b.s."

Pops clicked glasses with me, and we both took a big swallow of ignorant oil. Then Pops said: "That's the honest truth about that snake; that ain't no lie."

The jazz fans said, "Tell us about the snake!"

So Pops said, "As soon as me and Danny get another drink!" which he knew would annoy Nick.

"When I was a little boy in New Orleans," he began.

I chimed in, "Many, many years ago!" Everybody laughed and Nick smiled also.

"This is the honest to God truth," said Pops. "My family was living uptown on the outskirts of New Orleans, about a block from the Mississippi River. This section was not built up then and there were many open lots filled with tall weeds and grass. There were docks and wharves where small ocean-going fruit boats docked to unload their cargoes. The people in the neighborhood were in a panic, because babies, small children, goats, pigs, chickens, ducks, dogs and cats started disappearing. The police and city officials couldn't figure it out. They made many investigations but could find no clue to the mystery.

"The people in the neighborhood had been in the custom of getting up early, giving their children breakfast, feeding their pets and stock, and then turning them out to wander and roam about the area. But since the mysterious disappearances, they were in a panic and kept everything and everybody inside with the coming of nightfall: dogs, cats, goats and all.

"One morning a stevedore was going to work on the levee,

a dusky stevedore who was minding his business and in a very peaceful mood. He was a young man but suddenly he saw something that scared him so bad that the hair on his head turned snow white. I knew the man before this happened, when his hair was still black, but after this the people called him 'Snow White.'

"What he saw was a giant snake slowly crossing his path and when the snake saw him it slithered speedily past him into the high weeds. The stevedore was so scared that he couldn't move and when he came to his senses he ran back screaming, sweating and yelling at the top of his voice. A crowd gathered quickly and he told them about the big snake he saw. The news spread and the police were called. The police did not believe him, but he swore the snake was thirty feet long.

"A big police official told the stevedore, 'Boy, if you are lying about that snake I'm going to put you in jail.'

"The stevedore asked 'What for?'

"The law said, 'For telling a lie, creating a scene, disturbing the peace, malicious mischief and getting a mob of people on the public highways.'"

One of the jazz fans in the studio very seriously asked Pops, "Pops, did they have boy stevedores working on the levees in New Orleans during that time?"

Pops said, "No, but you see, white people in the South are in the habit of calling colored men 'boy' up to fifty years of age and if they think you are older than fifty they call you 'uncle'."

"Pops, is that a fact?" said the jazz fan.

Pops explained they also called colored women of different ages mammy, auntie and granny. It is their custom in the South. Then one of the engineers, annoyed at the interruption of of the tale said, "Pops, finish the story."

So Pops continued: "Well, the crowd became larger and larger and the stevedore kept swearing to the Lord that he was telling the truth. The fire engines came and the police, followed by the crowd, made the stevedore show them where he had seen the snake. Everybody had become very cautious because the size of the snake had reached huge proportions. The news spread that it was a dragon, a sea serpent, a monster and all sorts of terrifying things.

"The firemen and some brave men in the neighborhood started cutting and clearing the weeds and grass in the lot while the police held their guns drawn and after a while they saw a big hole in the ground. The snake man from the zoo rushed up, spoke to the police officials and it was decided that the snake would be captured alive.

"The officials had a big fire made to smoke the snake out. Meanwhile the crowd was yelling all shorts of advice, 'Shoot it!' and 'Hang it!' and they had all sorts of weapons: axes, hatchets, knives, razors, sticks and bricks. Then the firemen started to throw burning sticks and hot ashes from the fire down in the hole as the people kept their distance and watched anxiously. The stevedore was put into the patrol wagon and was crying like a baby because some of the crowd did not believe him and were calling him all sorts of nasty names.

"Suddenly someone yelled, 'There's the snake!'

"It was his head, but he went back down in the hole. Then the mob got out of hand but would not come near the hole. The snake man from the zoo stood over the hole with a rope lariat and after some more fire was thrown into the hole, the snake's head appeared again. The snake man lassoed it while some of the firemen and police caught hold of the rope and strained, trying to pull the snake out of the hole but the snake wouldn't budge. The crowd kept screaming but the snake man pleaded with the police not to shoot because this was a rare snake from South America, a giant Anaconda. After a while a cotton float came up, drawn by four big Missouri mules. The big colored driver unhitched the float and tied the rope to the harness on the mules.

"The police forced the people back and the mule driver popped his whip and the four mules strained and pulled the big snake out of the hole as the crowd screamed. After much tussling and wrestling with the wriggling snake, he was tied to the cotton float and taken to the zoo. The stevedore was turned loose and he was a hero in that section of the city of New Orleans. When he went into any saloon, the folks would say, 'Give Snow White a drink on me'."

I noticed that Nick was getting uneasy and salty so I said to Pops, "How did the snake get in this country?"

Pops said, "The people claimed that he must have come over here on one of those fruit boats on a bunch of bananas when he was very small."

Everybody in the studio was listening, looking at one another and Nick looked at Pops, then at me and shook his head as only he can. Then the jazz fan said, "When I go to New Orleans to the Mardi Gras next year, the first thing I'll do when I get there is to go to the zoo and see that snake."

Then Nick said, "Come on fellars! Come on fellars, let's finish this session."

Pops took a big drink and handed me the rest and I drank as we got in position and, as the signal lights started flashing, Pops said, "That's the God's honest truth."

The Creole songs recorded on this date, in June 1947, were: *Moi pas lemmé cas, Salée dame, Les oignons* and *Creole Blues*. This album appeared first on Circle records and then on the Riverside label.

4

The Red Light District

New Orleans throughout its history had, according to many noted authorities on the subject, just about the largest and most organized Red Light District in the Western hemisphere. Down through the years, the successive underworld king pins, from Jean Lafitte, the pirate, to the highly honored and respected Tom Anderson, owner of the Arlington Café, saw to it that men on the prowl in search of flesh and pleasure had and received their desire: providing they had the money to pay for it.

There were all sorts of establishments rigged up and operated for such activities, from the most elegant and palatial mansions to the most bare and decrepit cribs. A millionaire or a riverboat gambler with a trunk of greenbacks, or a lowly roustabout with a fifty-cent piece could and would obtain entertainment by just walking into a corner bar or barrelhouse and informing someone there of his desire. The city tolerated its famous District, and but for occasional threats of abolishing it every now and then, it was allowed to prosper side by side with sober and respectable citizens. The Red Light District was not just a small one or two square block community by the banks of the river or back by the tracks. Its location covered about two square miles of the center of the city from the Old Basin to the New Basin, from South Rampart Street to North Claiborne Avenue.

There were in this section small clusters of square blocks of decent people, but the majority of the inhabitants lived lustful lives or off the earnings of people who did. The tallest and largest buildings in the section were the Parish Prison and the Charity Hospital. Most of the jazz joints were scattered about here – that is cabarets, honky tonks, dives, sporting houses, gambling dens, Chinatown, four graveyards, the Pest House and a dozen pawn shops. The main drag for the Negro underworld was South Rampart Street and the side streets that crossed it: Perdido, Gasquet, Gravier, and the streets that ran parallel: Saratoga, Liberty, Howard and Villere and Robinson. Below Canal Street, which split the District in half, was Basin Street, which was noted for its famous and exclusive mansions, operated by such renowned women as Lulu White, Shaefer, Arlington, etc. On the other streets that ran parallel to Basin, Liberty, Marais, Villere, the class of the meat market prices descended as low as fifty cents for its entertainment. Also in this area there were two small narrow cobblestone one-and-two-block-long alleys close to Canal Street. There was Jane Alley, and below Canal Street there was Eclipse Alley, which ran into a dead end into New Orleans' oldest graveyard which holds the bones of Dominic You, Jean Lafitte, and also a huge mausoleum made of beautiful Italian marble. It was especially imported for an Italian benevolent society to bury their dead members.

In this area was also the Battlefield, and its name was appropriate. The Battlefield boasted dozens of New Orleans' most dangerous and ill-famed barrel houses, tonks, cribs and dives. Murders were common day and night occurrences. The cautious police patrolled the area in groups: couples, trios and quartets, and were careful not to blink an eye or relax. Before noon and up to about five p.m., the District, with the exception of restaurants, barber shops and small business places, had a very quiet and still atmosphere, almost deathlike – mainly because its inhabitants were asleep. There was not much stirring about; you saw maybe a streetwalker going to the store, or in and out of a dive or a tonk, but as if in a hurry or an emergency.

The bright sun or the broad daylight seemed to annoy them terribly. It was always in late evening near dusk or at nightfall when the district woke up, came to life, and its characters went on the prowl for fresh game. As night fell, the lights began to flicker on in the hundreds of dens, cribs and traps for the unwary. The joints began to get some action; as if out of nowhere there appeared, going to and fro to their neighborhood hangouts, dozens of whores, pimps, gamblers, hustlers and also all of the local characters who were physically able to move from their beds. When darkness finally settled on the District, it was like an amusement center: Coney Island, Atlantic City, boardwalk, music and laughter.

At its height, during the years 1850-1915, it boasted with pride, pomp and publicity, dozens of the most beautiful mansions in the Western hemisphere and nowhere in America were there to be found brothels rigged up to match them.

Side by side, or near them, stood hundreds of small bare cribs. The furniture in most of these small shacks, or small frame houses, consisted of just a bed or a couple of beds, two or three chairs and a few clothes hangers. There was always the strong poisonous odor of lye.

For their protection from the many customers who became violent or abusive or stubborn, many of the streetwalkers (the real professionals) kept an open can of lye which was partly filled with water. This caused the lye to boil. This lye was placed under the bed or in some handy place out of sight of the customers. Whenever a customer got an idea in his head that he would start some rough stuff, which many did, he suddenly found himself screaming, howling, jumping, and frantically trying to wipe the hot lye away from his face, chest, ears, eyes and the upper part of his body. These streetwalkers did not like to be beaten and abused and they never missed when they threw that lye.

When the victim finally arrived in the hospital, he was in bad shape and burnt up and in pain. The attendants at the emergency ward never rushed to attend the victim because they knew what the scoundrel had done. The lye never caused death, but it scarred a person for life. Most of the cribs adjoined other cribs and after the lye was hurled on a bully, the woman would hurry out the back door through the hole in the fence to the crib next door. She would hide out until the police relaxed or were taken care of. These women made it their practice to change cribs constantly and quite a few of the cribs were never occupied or used because they were considered to be bad luck or haunted, especially if a murder had been committed there.

The rent was cheap, many rented for as little as two dollars a week, mainly because no decent people would live there – that is, families. They were run down and ramshackle. The decent people who on rare occasions rented one were migrants from the small towns and plantations – escapees who came to New

Orleans penniless and were not in a position to be particular where they resided as long as there was a roof over their heads.

This was still the scene in the District when I was a small boy, in the days before Storyville was officially closed down. Poor children in New Orleans learned to hustle early, that is, to earn money. It was so in my youth, and I had very fine teachers, who were my two young uncles, Willie and Lucien. Willie was two years older than me, and Lucien was two years older than Willie.

From Friday after school until Saturday midnight, my two uncles, like most of the other poor boys, worked all kinds of hustles and chores to earn their spending money. These chores were selling papers, shining shoes, cleaning yards, selling brick, washing stoops (steps), and scrubbing banquettes (sidewalks). If it rained on the weekend and the above jobs were out, they worked the markets, that is, helping the women home with their market baskets.

The standard wage for most chores was five cents.

About selling brick, which was used by most housewives; I'll explain it. During the week, if you saw any building being demolished, you waited until the wrecking crew left. Then you pulled your wagon (most boys had home-made wagons) to the building and loaded it with a good supply of old, red soft clay bricks. You'd bring them home, get a flat stone and a hammer, soak the bricks in water and pound them to a powder, then go from door to door yelling, "Red brick for sale, lady!"

Most housewives bought this brick to sprinkle on and around their premises. It added color to the surroundings and it served another purpose if she was having domestic trouble or was superstitious. In such cases, to chase away bad luck or evil spirits, she moistened the brick with her urine and van van oil, that was sold at the Cracker Jack Drugstore on South Rampart Street. That drugstore sells everything used by the voodoo doctors, from snake hearts to frog titties.

There is a tenseness in the atmosphere on Saturday afternoons because most husbands get paid and if the head of the house is not home by six p.m., the wife is a nervous wreck. Wives are deeply grateful if a kid brings her husband home safely if he is drunk, helpless, and is staggering home, and many husbands staggered home on weekends.

My two uncles were champs at peeping into bar-rooms and checking on the habitual weekend juiceheads. When I was about seven years old, my uncle Willie got a job on an icewagon one Saturday as a helper, so I borrowed his shoeshine box and he schooled me how to hustle shines. He said to walk up Burgundy Street, go in all the bar-rooms, tonks and gambling joints, look sad and ask all the men if they would like a shine. Always ask the drunken men first, because, he said, when a man is drunk ,he feels sorry for poor children and he remembers when he was small, and he wants to show off and be a big shot.

I follow his instructions, and I am doing okay.

I pass St. Ann Street and about the middle of the block I hear a piano in a house, playing the horses. (That's what people in New Orleans called boogie woogie, because it was the same thing over and over and sounded like a gang of horses trotting.) I stopped and listened.

After a while, a very pretty lady opened the door and said, "Garçon, will you go to the grocery for me?"

She spoke in creole patois, and I said, "Yes, ma'am."

I noticed she had on a pretty silk negligée, all full of ribbons and flowers. She handed me a dollar and said, "Get me two kinds of bacon, two dozen eggs and a French bread. Leave your shoeshine box with me, and when you come back, come through the alley, and I'll be in the kitchen."

I hurried to the grocery and bought food: eggs, twenty cents a dozen; bacon, fifteen cents a pound, and the French bread, three cents. The clerk gave me half a stage plank when I asked for a lagniappe. Lagniappe is a tip or token kids receive for patronizing the store. A stage plank is a ginger cake, three inches wide, six inches long, a half-inch thick, and the top is sugar-coated.

I hurried back with the groceries and went in the alley. About midway I heard the piano player rolling the horses. My curiosity got the better of me, so I stopped and peeped through the Venetian style door. It was daylight and the sun was shining brightly, but in the room where I was looking I saw a very exciting scene. There was a red light on, and sitting around were about ten men and women, laughing, talking, drinking, smoking and having a good time. In the center of the room, a fine-built woman was doing the naked dance in the nude. I was shocked at first, but I stayed there with my eyes glued on the scene.

The woman who sent me to the store came into the room and whispered something to the woman who was doing the dance. She stopped dancing, the pianist stopped playing, looked around surprised, and there was silence within as the naked woman sat on the knee of one of the men.

With the show ended, I went back to the kitchen and delivered the groceries. The woman handed me my shinebox and said angrily, "Skidoo! Smarty!" She handed me a dime. I didn't care about her being angry because I could hear the piano playing the horses again.

I walked back through the alley to the door and started looking at the naked dance that was in progress again.

Suddenly from above, it seemed like Niagara Falls was pouring down on me, and the liquid had a very strong odor! I recognized it quickly, and while I'm wiping my eyes, face, ears and hands, I hear the woman who sent me to the grocery store say, "I fixed that cheeky little bastard! I went upstairs and drowned him in a pot of stale piss!"

One of the men said, "You gave him the Golden Shower!" Everybody in the room started laughing.

I went out the gate and walked home in the street, and not on the sidewalk. I was so ashamed, as I thought people might smell me.

In later years, after I had started playing music, I recognized her at a cabaret. We were in the same party and were introduced, so I said, "I know you."

"I don't know you!" she said.

Then I said, "I met you years ago."

She said, "I don't remember seeing you before."

So I whispered to her where I met her and she laughed herself into hysterics. Everybody wanted to know what was so funny and I said, "Tell 'em!"

She did, and everyone laughed.

She said, "You broke up that party, and I was sorry after. One of the men followed you home, thinking you'd tell your mother or the police!"

I asked her, "Who was the piano player?"

She said, "That was Tanglefoot Joe Robichaux – you know, Joe Draggers."

* * *

There were always plenty of laughs on the New Orleans jazz scene for there were many comical characters. I remember a banjo player rushing to my home one Friday afternoon. His name was Peter Poppy. He said, "Son, I want you to go and play in my place tonight at the Olympia Hall."

I agreed to go. He said, "Just tell the fellows I sent you."

I went to the hall that night. The leader was called Freddie Boo-Boo. He played fine trombone. We started to play at 9.00 p.m. All the five members of this band were old pros and played the songs called by Mr. Boo-Boo in the jazz tradition. I was not introduced to the other musicians – Mr Boo-Boo must have felt that we knew one another. After the second intermission I was congratulated by the musicians because I played the songs well, and they had never seen me before. The introductions went like this:

"Kid, meet Mr Buddy Zuzu." (He was the bass player.)

"Meet Mr. Blind Freddie." (The clarinetist.)

"Meet Mr. Black Happy." (The drummer.)

"Meet Mr. Shots Madison." (The cornetist.)

Then Mr. Boo-Boo himself said, "And my name is Freddie Boo-Boo!"

I didn't show my amusement, but it struck me as funny to see how each of the men was known by a colorful nickname, but displayed no resentment.

Later, I made a list of the names and nicknames of characters who were a part of the New Orleans scene. Some were before my time, some were real life legends, and some I knew by being a musician. These people were a constant topic of conversation on bandstands and in places of pleasure. In fact they were the local celebrities.

The women included Flaming Mamie, Crying Emma, Bucktown Bessie, Mary Meathouse, Ida Crocket, Gold Tooth Gussie, Big Butt Annie, Struttin' Stella, No Leg Mary, Kidney Foot Rella, Baldhead Bea, Minnie Ha Ha, Black Ann, Larceny Hearted Ann, Lil Sis, Sophie Satterfield, Ella Ludlow, Naked Mouf Mattie, Bird Leg Nora, Sweet Lucy, Ready Money, Coke Eye Laura, Pretty Christine, One Arm Edna, Daisy Parker, Lotsa Mamma, Tish-Tishamingo, Black Bess, Miss Thing, Ida Jackson, Yellow Gal, Pretty Brown, Black Sis, Tee Fee, Merriney Ethel, Lily The Crip, Red Lite Hester, Ann Cook, Mary Jack The Bear.

Lee Collins mentioned all these women when I was a member of his band. He'd be talking about their deeds and misdeeds. Albertina McKay, for example, was Joe Lindsay's old lady. One day she started screaming. She was a cop-caller. Her old man gets home to find her squatted down and screaming, "Here come the po-lice!"

She was mad at him because he had gone across the river, so she was going to have somebody locked up for molesting her, or claiming they'd molested her, just to get back at him.

Cuby Doll, Pretty Lil, Struttin' Lilly, Black Mag, Ratty Rita, Suzie Sutton, Peacherino, these were all women of the tenderloin. All these characters had names based on the deeds they had done to earn them notoriety.

Among the men of the District, Robert Charles was supposed to have shot nine policemen. He wasn't a bad man, but the police messed with him. He ran off and got some ammunition and they ambushed him. He was quite a marksman with the rifle he had and he just started shooting! There's a helluva story behind that day when he was shooting policemen.

Aaron Harris was a rough man.

Seymour Clay got in trouble with the city government and the politicians. I'm not sure quite what happened to him, but I think he was hanged.

Then there were more characters like Slippers, Darbee,

Dirty Dog, Steel Arm Johnny, Julius Sands, Boxcar Shorty and Willie Blue – those were the two that Cousin Joe sang that song about. Then there were Jean Pierre and Honoré. They were two activists way back in the days of the District who got in trouble with the politicians. They were campaigning for rights for black people, the right to vote. They had creole names, they were very aggressive, but they ended up getting in trouble.

Then there was Joe Rucker, Knock on The Wall, Boar Hog and Tudlum. Tudlum was the boss of the District for a while. I remember him because he had a joint called Tudlum's Tonk. I used to play in there with that little kids' band I had, the Bouzan Kings. He let us play a few numbers and then pass the hat. Tudlum always had on new clothes. I don't know why, but always his collars looked like they were too big with the wrong knot tied. It was all new stuff, but he'd buy oversize.

Then there was Low Gravy and Black Satin. Satin was a prizefighter, and I remember his uncle used to have a joint where he sold reefers. There was Uncle Rat and Chick Leg Horace, also known as One Leg Horace. Although Horace only had one leg, he was the king of the second-liners at street parades, and he led his unwelcome hordes of celebrants at all kinds of funerals and other parades. Eventually he retired because of his health, but he could keep up a fair turn of speed on his wooden leg, which looked a bit like an upturned stool.

Spy Boy was the name given to the man who was the spy, or look-out, for one of the societies of Mardi Gras Indians.

Then there were Big Stack and Little Stack, Kitestick – who was a ball player – and Eightball. Eightball was a District character named after the black ball in the pool game. The black ball with a little white spot on where you can see the number. They called him "Eightball" because he was really black – they didn't ever call him "Redball" or "Third ball", just Eightball, and that means you're black. Some bad cat called him that name and it stuck, so he had to go for it.

Titanic was gay. He was the District's most famous homosexual. He had a whole lot of homosexual friends who dressed as women and hustled as women, even back in the twenties. I guess that's been going on since Nero's time. There was a tonk in the District where I was playing once called the Boudoir, and that was famous as the hangout of all the queers and faggots who lived in the District.

I first met a young man called Dejan there. He could have been related to the musical Dejan family, like Harold who led the Olympia Band or his brother Leo, but this Dejan was brown, not light-skinned like them.

Dejan was one of the most fearless fellows I ever saw in a fracas. He was a nice looking man when I met him, of about twenty five years and he weighed about one hundred and fifty pounds. Amongst the gamblers about town he was highly respected. Among the smart boys it was an accepted fact that Dejan knew all the slick tricks at cheating with dice, cards, pool and billiards. Dejan was not a big man but he was reputed to have fought and whipped quite a few bad men.

Dejan loved music. He bought a gold-plated banjo. It was decorated all over with mother-of-pearl and semi-precious stones, and was the prettiest banjo that I have ever seen.

In the rear of the Boudoir there was a gambling den and Dejan was running the games. I would play there on Friday, Saturday and Sunday with a trio. The first Friday night, Dejan, not busy in the gambling den, came over to the bandstand, complimented us and watched me play. He said, "Gee, I wish you would show me how to strum my banjo and make that figure of eight stroke."

During the break, we went into the stockroom and I showed and taught Dejan the figure of eight stroke. He was thrilled. The next night I let him play a few tunes with the trio: *It Ain't Gonna Rain No More* and *Who's Sorry Now?* After that, Dejan was my number one fan.

The Boudoir was a new scene and experience to me. These people were something to see. I had heard of and seen grown men and boys who were feminine, who acted girlish and womanish, but I had never seen a compact group of such people all together at the same time.

I was hired by a fine jazz pianist named Georgie Parker,

who liked the way I would follow his chord patterns. We'd been in a near-death duel previously, which had taken place on a boat, but Georgie Parker did not bear me any grudge.

One Saturday, we had played at a village called Violet, Louisiana, which was down below New Orleans. At about four p.m. that evening, we sailed down there on a small fishing boat on the Mississippi River. The trip had been a pleasant one, but on our return trip against the current, the boat had a trying time fighting the rough Mississippi. At one point a large ship which was traveling downstream on its way to the Gulf of Mexico passed our boat and the Captain of the smaller vessel yelled in some seaman's lingo, "Hold fast!"

We were sitting on the rear deck, Georgie, Black Norman and myself. Norman and I had been friends since childhood. When the big ship passed, the after-waves caused the little boat almost to capsize. Norman and Georgie grabbed something to hold on to and I laughed as I grabbed at my banjo and a rope or a rail. The boat's crew seemed to know about this situation – a large ship passing a small boat. If we went overboard, it would have been a common scene to the Mississippi River seamen. They'd have reported when the small boat docked, "One or two niggers lost!"

The small boat rocked and rolled, almost capsizing. This went on for about ten minutes. I laughed and Norman joined in the laughter which made Georgie Parker furious. He was terrified and began to curse me, calling me all sorts of uncouth names.

I noticed that the passengers on the large ship were on the rear deck and laughed at us on our little boat. When the boat finally stopped rocking and rolling, Georgie threatened to whip me and Norman, and he told me so as he swore to the heavens that he would never hire me again as long as he lived. It was okay with me.

We landed and departed. The next Friday he came to my house and asked me to play at this joint in the Red Light District called Beansy's Boudoir.

I reminded him of the incident on the boat and he replied, "Man, I done forgot all about that."

So I took the job. With us was another drummer, Morris

Morand, who was Lizzie Miles's kid brother. His nickname was Magee – he was a very hot-tempered youngster who would fight at the drop of a hat. We became fast friends.

Magee was playing at a house party one Saturday night, just piano and drums. He got into an argument with one of the male guests, grabbed a kerosene lamp and threw it at the man. The lamp shattered against the wall and set the wall on fire. There was a stampede and pandemonium as the guests ran into the street. Quick action by some cool-headed individual, who doused the fire, averted the flames from burning the house down. After that Magee was highly respected by everybody.

So, Georgie, Magee and I opened that Friday night. This was during the summer of 1926. We started to play at ten p.m. on a very small bandstand near the bar, where we could view the entire scene. I noticed that the bartenders, waitresses and everyone in the joint was acting very womanish. The old folks in New Orleans called such feminine-acting men "moffydice" – slang for the word "hermaphrodite."

The few weekends that I worked at the Boudoir, the people were crammed and jammed like sardines in a can. Each night there were present about two hundred sissies, faggots, punks, moffydice, she-men and she-boys – all colors, all sizes and all ages (from sixteen to sixty.) They were high-class, low-class, well-dressed, ragged, dignified, loud-mouthed – all talking at the same time, running to and fro, hither and yon. They would all talk and gossip about each other, just like women do. There were men who dressed in women's clothes, and these came in after midnight. They wore make-up and looked just like women.

There was one who claimed she was pregnant and was going to have a baby. One old sissy said, real loud, when the fat-bellied sissy came into the joint, "When is that lying bitch going to have her baby? Her belly has been puffed up for almost twenty months now. She must be gonna have a baby elephant."

All those sissies did was to drink and gossip about each other in a very vulgar fashion.

While I played, I sat on a fairly high bar stool, parallel to the bar and near the entrance. I had a good view of the whole scene. I watched the gay girls as they came in and as they left and I watched them talk at the bar. I saw them and heard their caustic remarks about others, and I saw them hunch one another as they gossiped.

Dejan said, "Danny, if you will show me something more about the banjo, I'll pay you and teach you to gamble."

I said, "I'll show you what little I know, but I don't care for gambling."

Dejan said, "Look! I keep a pocket full of money, and you could do the same." He showed me a big roll of money. "You can gamble for a living and play the banjo on the side. Come into the back room and watch the game when you have your inter-mission."

So, to please him, I went in the gambling room, watched a while and then left.

The next night I went back to the gambling room. As I walked in I heard an argument. A gambler was cursing Dejan and denying that he had cheated. Dejan said, "No man living and born from a meat woman is going to curse me!"

Fast as a cat, Dejan grabbed the gambler's right hand and jerked his arm violently while throwing a deck of cards in the man's face. The gambler grabbed for his shoulder which was very painful. Then Dejan grabbed a chair and pulled a leg off. The other gamblers scattered like birds as he proceeded to beat the gambler. I walked out of the room and back to the bandstand. I heard the gambler begging Dejan to please stop beating him but I continued to hear blows and finally I heard the gambler moan, "Please! Don't kill me!"

The sissies started to scream, and I have never heard such screaming from that day to this. "Murder! They're killing a man back there! Help! Police!"

From the back room came, "Have mercy! Someone save me! God have mercy! Jesus save me! Somebody help me! Please save me!"

I just sat on the stool looking at this mad scene and I noticed that not one of the sissies ran out into the street; they just stood and screamed like a bunch of hens in a barnyard – some were

111

squatting, some holding their breasts, some screaming up to the ceiling.

This screaming built up to a contest with everyone trying to outscream the other. I looked at all this compact variety of sissies, screaming at the tops of their voices – screaming blue murder (which means until they were blue in the face – that is the light colored ones.) There were all sorts of high-pitched voices – lyric sopranos, mezzo sopranos, coloratura sopranos, canary sopranos and a few ancient sissies who tried hard, but since their voices were gone they just wheezed.

Dejan walked out of the gambling room. He was covered in blood – the gambler's blood. The faggots continued to scream and yell at the tops of their voices.

Dejan heard all this screaming and jumped up on the bar. He grabbed two bottles of whisky from the back of the bar and reared back wildly as if to throw them at the crowd. He loudly yelled, "You bitches! Shut up this mother so-and-so noise!"

Suddenly there was quiet. Everybody calmed down and resumed their gossiping and drinking as if nothing had happened. A group of men then carried the beaten gambler out of the Boudoir because he could not walk, his legs were in such bad shape. They took him over to the hospital and told the policeman on duty that a truck had run over him.

Then they returned to the Boudoir to give the doctor's report on the gambler's condition:

> two broken arms (above the elbow);
> two broken legs (below the knee);
> and a broken collarbone.

A sissy found the gambler's false teeth. Dejan said, "Give them to me! I'll take them to the hospital."

And so he did, the very next day.

* * *

When you saw Dejan, you just took it easy, you didn't go running, running. Timon was another bad young man. When I say bad, these were street brawlers. They didn't shoot anybody, they just used their fists.

Bang Zang was a guy with legs that made him walk oddly, knock-kneed. He was one of the second-liners on parades who carried a big stick. There were three brothers, Big Bang, Little Bang and Bang Zang, who got his name because of his "Bang-Zang legs." They all used to second-line, but none so much as him. His big stick was a spoke out of a wagon-wheel. He'd whirl it so he could hit you across the shins.

Butterfoot was another bad man, so was Red Cap, a real rough character, and Sweet Honey was another one. Walter Bell was real rough, and Son Saw, like Titanic, was homosexual.

There was a man called Copper Cent. He went to the penitentiary for what seemed like twenty years. Eventually he came back. He was a quiet sort of guy, but he had stolen something with his brothers, and he was sent down for a long time and served it to the day.

Sore Dick was a common name, but my uncles knew a particular guy with this name. All these people were living people, these lists of names, who were part of the life of the District and stayed on in the area after Storyville closed.

There was a man who lived in the seventh ward (that's downtown, where I was reared,) who would and did annoy me and the other boys and the old folks many times. He was General Zachariah, a fat, dark man who weighed about three-hundred pounds. He was very active for his age (when I knew him, he was about forty-five years old or maybe more.) He would dress in a military uniform which consisted of an admiral's hat with a large ostrich plume on the top, a long, blue general's coat of the Union forces, and gray Confederate Army pants with stripes down the sides. His entire chest was completely covered with all sorts of medals and ribbons, and he would parade about the street during the afternoon like a Grand Marshall. He would strut very proudly – waving his arms and kicking up his feet – remindful of gymnastic exercises.

This strangely attired character led a three-piece military group – a fife or flute or clarinet, a huge bass drum beater and a snare drummer similar to the Uncle Sam posters. He would be advertising some local store sale, while two boys followed holding up a large cloth banner or sign which described the sale – where and when the sale would be. Sometimes it was a grocery store, hardware, clothing store or it might be a market. A half dozen boys would pass out handbills to the housewives who came to their front porches and doors to see him and the excitement he created. He always did create a scene and plenty of excitement because a hundred or more small children followed him – in a happy "second line."

The musicians played but two pieces – the first dozen bars of *Dixie* and a part of the *Battle Hymn of the Republic* –one after the other. They played them over and over. He paraded just about a half dozen squares from the business place which he was promoting, zig-zagging the blocks.

He was very comical – but in a serious sort of way. He never smiled or laughed but acted the part of a real stern military general.

The people indoors would hear the extra loud bass drum and then rush out to the street, expecting to see a big parade or a procession – then they would look on, disenchanted, as he passed.

He was very clever. His uniform showed him to be a neutral about the Civil War.

* * *

Good Lord the Lifter was another well-known young man in the downtown section of New Orleans. The eminent Mr. Lifter, from a very early age, had an honest and sincere belief that anything of commercial value that was not locked up or nailed down and laying around idly, belonged to him, especially if there was no one in the immediate vicinity of the object he was eyeballing. And there was a reason for his attitude.

As far back as Mr. Lifter could remember he had existed from day to day by taking anything within his reach to eat and nourish his body. I asked an old musician who knew Lifter's folks and his environment. The musician told me that Lifter's folks were very poor people. He was the surviving brother of fraternal twins. For some reason, when he and his brother were about six, his brother suddenly decided that he would not eat anything offered him, and slowly starved to death.

Lifter lived in a tenement with his mother, his grandmother and his mother's two sisters. His mother and grandmother were widows. His two aunts were young women, not married. His mother, grandmother, and his aunts just did not seem to get along with men. They all worked for well-to-do and wealthy white folks as cooks and housekeepers. Lifter constantly heard the grievances of his folks, especially at suppertime. As was the custom, and still is, the white folks' servants worked late but went to work early, from seven or eight a.m. till seven at night, but they were allowed to take home the leavings from the table and icebox. Lifter's folks brought him the best and choicest foods and desserts and showered him with affection because he was the only male in the family. He was the apple of their eye.

As Lifter sat around the dinner table at night, he heard all sorts of stores, tragic and funny, that his grandmother, mother and aunts related to one another. Lifter was allowed to hear these stories because it is the belief in New Orleans, "Let them children know so they won't be no damned fools."

I had the pleasure of knowing this teenage youngster who was given the nickname Mr. Good Lord the Lifter. I never knew him in a personal way because he did not seem to value or encourage personal, intimate or confidential friendship. I never saw him with a group of boys or with anyone. He was always alone – walking slowly, going about his business. When I first saw, heard and was told about him, he was about sixteen years of age. Very dark, about near six feet tall. He was fairly good looking, with a round, dimpled face with two extra-large clear bright white eyes. His eyes were like owl's, staring and continuously shifting slyly in every direction.

I saw him many times. He never smiled or frowned; his dark, smooth face was like a mask. When he'd slowly pass a group of men or boys, there was mischievous laughter as someone greeted him: "Hey, Good Lord!" or "Here comes the Lifter."

He never answered vocally but he bowed slightly or lifted

his hand and continued on his way. Mr. Lifter was not a school-boy. He was one of the many youngsters who just were seen all about town doing nothing. Just walking and sitting about, in deep meditation, like a hawk on a fence or in a tree, watching a barn-yard or hen house. Whenever you saw these boys and men on a scene you looked about them to see what was near of commercial value.

Louis Armstrong recorded a song entitled *Drop that Sack.*

There was another young man who was called just that – but with dialect – "Drop dat sack." He was also always on the move or prowl. The New Orleans police always stopped men and boys who carried sacks over their shoulders to see what was inside the sacks. If a crowd of people did not gather around, the sack carrier was kicked in the behind and warned as the police drove off with the sack and its contents.

I learned that Mr. Good Lord the Lifter at an early age felt, as I said, anything laying about unused belonged to him.

After thinking about Good Lord and his tactics, I once asked a proud and boastful thief why he stole. He told me, laughingly, whoever owns something and is not using it and is letting it lie around carelessly, must not care too much about it. So since he must not value the article, he don't need it.

Mr. Lord performed two very humorous thefts that gave him fame and the name "Good Lord the Lifter."

The first was this. He passed one of New Orleans' largest funeral parlors which was located in the Garden District, the wealthy section of the city. He was walking up St. Charles Street slowly when he passed the undertaking parlor. He slowed down his pace and looked into the large display room adjoining the parlor. Through the large plate glass window he saw inside a dozen or so expensive metal coffins and caskets. The caskets fascinated him, so he just stood there staring at them and watching the lifeless stillness of the large room. Good Lord stood there a long time. He looked at the large clock and timed his careful observation. He noticed that passers-by hurried past the large establishment and never looked twice at the caskets, because people don't like to look at coffins or at funeral parlors. He also noticed that no one connected with the funeral parlor entered the display room, especially since it was around lunch time. Good Lord saw that the door was opened wide and the large floor was covered with thick plush carpeting as he counted the coffins and slowly walked off.

The next day, about the same time, Good Lord arrived at the large window of the funeral parlor display room and stood silently watching the large clock and the interior. This day Good Lord carried a good sized potato sack and a couple of screwdrivers. After carefully making sure all was quiet and nothing was stirring about, he walked inside to the rear, got on his knees, and silently started unscrewing the beautiful handles off the caskets and coffins. After one hour of noiseless screwing, Good Lord walked out of the room with a sack heavily loaded with coffin handles. He walked straight to another famous gentleman's business concern: John Quee, pronounced by the people in patois: Jean Kwee.

Jean Kwee was a very prosperous junk dealer, or, as they say in New Orleans – a junkman. He had a large junkyard in the downtown Creole section, near the Old Basin and a block or so from Good Lord's home. He was an old white man who wore a black derby hat, a gingham shirt, and dark baggy oversized, greasy, dirty pants held up by suspenders. He was reputed to dislike water, bathtubs and especially soap. I saw him many times and at first I thought he was a colored man because he was so dark, but I noticed that he had blue eyes.

I angered him one day by staring closely at his face. He frowned and said "What"s the matter?"

I said, "Nothing!" but never went there again.

He was way up in age, maybe sixty, short, and his face and neck were deeply creased with many wrinkles. In these many wrinkles was dirt that had accumulated. He probably bathed now and then but he never scraped the soil from these wrinkled furrows. When Mr. Good Lord walked in the junk yard and laid his loot on the table, Mr. Kwee smiled and said, "What you got for me today?"

Good Lord, wearily panting, replied, "I got seventy-two

handles.

Mr. Kwee asked, "What kind of handles?"

Good Lord said, "All kinds, gold, silver, brass – all kinds."

"Handles from what?" Mr. Kwee asked.

Good Lord replied, wearily, "Handles, handles."

When Mr. Kwee reached in the sack and started taking out the handles, he was stunned and surprised. He said, "My boy, these are coffin handles."

Good Lord said, "What's wrong with that?"

Mr. Kwee said, "Nothing, where did you get them?"

"I found them at an undertaker parlor uptown on St. Charles Street.

"St. Charles and what?"

"The one with that large clock in front of it."

Mr. Kwee, rubbing his gray haired chin, smiled and said, "I know the place."

Good Lord said, "How much are the handles worth?"

"I'll give you twenty five cents apiece for them."

"All right, give me the money."

Mr. Kwee counted the handles and paid Good Lord his money. Good Lord put the money in his pocket and said, "Thanks, Mr. Kwee."

Mr. Kwee said "Nice work, my boy. Stay out of that neighborhood and also off the street and don't wear them clothes you got on for a month or so."

A week later, Mr. Kwee called the owner of the funeral parlor and whispered, "Do you know anyone who would be interested in buying a mass of brand new coffin handles?"

It is the custom of firemen after returning from a fire to place the wet water house on a ramp outside of the fire house to let the water run out and to dry. After the fire the fireman are generally exhausted so after the hose is put on the ramp they retire inside and relax and sleep. It does not take much imagination to work out the next item to appear at Jean Kwee's junkyard in the hands of Mr. Good Lord The Lifter.

* * *

There is a term used in underground circles: "hustler." When a man noted as such is arrested by the police and booked at the police station, the first charge against him is "having no visible means of support." The second is "D and S," (dangerous and suspicious.) Being a grown man and having no job or means of support and being a habitué of notorious dens and dives, the hustler is looked upon with suspicion. "If he ain't working he must be stealing!"

Such a man was Stack o' Dollars. He had no love for manual labor. He was always neat but rarely dressed up. He'd been arrested countless times but released when he explained that he had a leaking heart. He was never caught but it was rumored that he was a "gown man." A gown man was a robber. They were plentiful around New Orleans. They dressed in women's clothes and late in the night they hid in the dark and waylaid people.

Stack, as he was called, lived with a woman called Sugar Lou. They had a fracas and Stack beat her up real bad. He blackened her eyes and broke her arm and left her for dead. About a week later she found him in a bar-room and another fight occurred. She was beaten and almost killed again. Stack left her lying on the floor and went out the door.

A few days passed and she saw him go into another dive. She went and found a policeman who was a noted nigger-killer. She told him about Stack's cruelty and the numerous beatings he had given her.

They went to the dive where Stack was. When Stack saw Sugar Lou and the police, he ran out of the side door. The policeman followed Stack, shooting. Stack fell and rolled over on his side, groaning. He attempted to rise but fell into a fairly deep gutter, face first.

He tried to rise again but weakened. His head submerged and bubbles were seen to rise out of the nasty, slimy, green stagnant water. The cop stood above Stack with his gun. Sugar Lou stood beside him cursing Stack who laid still in the gutter. When the ambulance and the patrol wagon both arrived some men pulled Stack out of the gutter and laid him on his back. The intern examined Stack and pronounced him dead. At the morgue, when the coroner examined the body and signed the death certificate, it read "Cause of death: drowning." The bullet did not cause his death. Stack's lungs were full of green, slimy gutter water.

After that, Sugar Lou became one of the most despised women in New Orleans. She had become what is known and hated in the underworld – a "cop-caller" – that is an unforgivable sin. There are two types of rats the underworld despises: the stool pigeons and the cop-callers. The adage of the underworld is "we settle our own disputes."

* * *

The ladies of the District, who were not too proud to wear hand-me-downs, were never in need of fine, exquisite, delicate, expensive, beautiful underthings, because there was a well-known shoplifter, who, warned by the police that he would be sent up the river if he were caught for the hundredth time after ninety-nine offenses, then introduced the fine art of yard-lifting.

When Mr. Rough Dry Sammy received the stern warning from the judge not to come before him again for shoplifting, Sammy mastered the art of yard-lifting.

What was so unique about Rough Dry Sammy was not his clever method of yard-lifting, but his masterful method of subduing bad vicious dogs. Sammy could approach the meanest dogs, kneel, call softly to them, and they would come as happily as if he was their master. Sammy could imitate the bark or growl of any dog, whether it was a large Airedale or a tiny Pekingese lapdog. If a group of neighborhood mongrels, which were commonly called "kiyoodles," were playing in the street and Sammy had never seen them before, he could approach them, bark, and they would all stop playing and look at him amazed. Then they looked at one another in shocked surprise.

As most dogs of different breeds and sizes have different barks of varied volume, when Rough Dry Sammy would walk in the midst of a group of dogs and kneel, he would growl and pat each dog individually. As each dog barked, Sammy would bark in perfect imitation. He could bark to a particular dog as the others watched his every move, and the dog would run off speedily to its house.

He could give forth a series of barks and the pack of dogs would scamper off in all directions to their homes. He could stand on a corner and bark loudly, and in a few seconds all the dogs in the neighborhood could be heard, yelping their loudest.

When Rough Dry Sammy was in a happy mood there was a funny prank he would pull, which was of great annoyance to housewives. As is the custom in respectable neighborhoods, folks keep pet dogs who are loved as members of the family. Also, it is the custom of these folks to sit on their porches in the afternoon, with their pet dogs lying around and about in quiet contentment.

Sammy would pass these porches, looking straight ahead, as though he saw no-one, give forth a soft growl or bark, and the dog would leap from the side of its master and follow Sammy to his rear fence or six feet. The surprised dog owner would call and call and call, but the dog would follow Sammy, completely ignoring its master.

Many an owner of pedigreed dogs would rush onto the sidewalk, frantically calling after a prize pet who was disappearing into the distance. Then he would have to rush inside his house to dress decently enough to take up the chase after his pet.

As Rough Dry Sammy walked along, other dogs would join in the parade. The dog owners came running behind, followed by kids from the neighborhood. Sammy would bark, never looking back and the dogs would start a loud barking battle among themselves, with Sammy going about his business.

Whenever Rough Dry Sammy was broke and in need of a few dollars, he would call the medical schools in New Orleans and ask if they needed any dogs for experiments in their laboratories. If so, he would put on his pied piper routine – that is, start walking casually to the medical school, and by the time he arrived, following behind him were as many dogs as they needed. One afternoon, in front of one of New Orleans' leading department stores, in a big expensive sports car, driven by a uniformed chauffeur, sat a very dignified, aristocratic, cultured white lady. In her lap was a little Pekingese dog which she was fondly stroking.

Sammy passed by, saw the peaceful scene, walked about fifty feet, stopped, turned around and traced his steps back past the big car. As he passed by, he barked softly in a high-pitched range. The little Pekingese dog started barking frantically and jumped out of his mistress's lap. He would not allow her or the chauffeur to touch or to quieten him. The Pekingese kept up the barking until it had drawn a large crowd. Seems like the message the dog received from Rough Dry Sammy must have caused him suddenly to acquire a deep, bitter hatred for his mistress.

The little dog kept up the racket, and finally the embarrassed lady told her chauffeur, "Please hurry up and drive us to the veterinarian, my poor little dog has gone crazy!" And the car sped off.

Rough Dry Sammy's racket did not make sense to me because, as clever as he was at handling dogs, I wondered why he did not become a dog trainer, or get himself a dog act and go on stage. But like most clever people in the underworld, they just don't want to do things honest and legitimate.

Sammy or his wife would be seen in the dives and joints in the District, with paste board boxes of ladies' underthings that he had pilfered from the back yards of New Orleans' leading wealthy folks. Sammy would make the round in the rich neighborhoods and quietly, while the people were having their evening siesta in the cool of their homes, he would empty their clothes lines and fill his sack with their fancy, expensive underwear.

On countless occasions, many of the city's aristocratic ladies suddenly found themselves drawerless. Many went to glamorous social affairs with their bottoms bare to the damp, chilly night air.

Rough Dry Sammy's wife, who was an excellent laundress, ironed and pressed these underthings until they looked new. Then she, or Sammy, made the rounds of the joints, selling them to the women of the District.

In the year 1940, while on a visit to New Orleans, I inquired about Rough Dry Sammy. I was shown a small store front church of which Rough Dry Sammy had become the pastor. A sign on the front read: "Reverend Robert Wilson – Minister."

5
Houses of Ill Repute

Now about these good time houses. In different parts of the country they are called by different names – but it's all the same. In New Orleans – a sporting house, in Chicago – a buffet flat, in New York City – a joint, in Boston and the East – a house of assignation.

In my travels as a musician there was always a house or houses where a musician, performer, railroad man, seaman, gambler or, as was the case – anyone who was on the road or on the bum, was welcomed with outstretched arms. I say it like that because that was the way you were greeted when you knocked on the door and the proprietress greeted you. That is, if you could say or give an honest answer when you were asked who sent you. When on the road, constantly eating in greasy spoons (cheap cafes, Greek restaurants, Chinese restaurants,) you quickly got tired of eating the same fare. In my case when it happened to me, I'd calmly and casually ask a cab driver, railroad man, porter or someone who looked smart, "Say Pops" or "Old Man" (a bill of money helped,) "Where can I go where there's some action?" or "Where can I find an after-hour joint?" or "Who is the nicest landlady 'round town where I can have some fun?"

The people who owned or promoted these places, in spite of being located and scattered all over the country, were definitely of the same breed or made of the same type of flesh. If you once learned the art of getting along with one, you could get along with them all. They have, in most cases, the same personality with a slight variance now and then. They all seemed to have very little fear of the law or the police; they all seemed to have had at times in the past skirmishes with the police. They rarely do or did much talking and if they do or did it was only when the business is prospering. If they know you are a stranger and just passing through for a short while (that is, if you meet their approval,) you are told to make yourself at home. After you are okayed you can become very annoying if you are polite about making yourself at home, such as asking, "Where's the phone?" "Where's the bathroom?" "Where are the glasses?"

I was told, scores of times, "Man, get off your ass. There's the phone – over there. There's the glasses on the shelf – the bathroom is up the hall."

Always with this disgusted final remark, "God damn, you been coming 'round here two days – and you still don't know where nothing's at – where's your eyes, in your ass?"

They are not angry. They are just lazy and don't want to be annoyed as they seem to be tired physically. I figured it out: their cross attitude was just a result of their suffering from a chronic case of nervous tension – just plain old (rest broken.) Then, these places are generally open twenty-four hours around the clock. Visitors are never turned away, even if they are they are pests, loudmouths, deadbeats and bums. The center of activities is always in the kitchen or dining room, and all the talk and drinking is done at or around a large table. If you have passed the careful scrutiny of the owner and the clique of regular clients, you will soon hear many weird tales and all the current gossip of the underworld and night life.

You will have been asked, unbeknowing to yourself, some times before by the owner – "Where did you say you are from?"

In my case, when I heard that question, I'd say rather proudly, "I'm from New Orleans."

That meant I was accepted like a long-lost relative. I'd make it my business, when there was a quorum around the table, to relate some fantastic tale: a tragedy, something that involved murder, jail, romance, voodoo, gambling, graveyards, music, whores and pimps and end with the killing of a rotten stool pigeon or a mean policeman. I'd always tell the tale without a smile, and in sympathy with the gambler, whore, pimp; describing the death struggle, weapon, blood all over the place and on many occasions when I'd extend the tale to the burial of the principal characters and the minute details of bodies in coffins in the funeral homes, I'd pause and watch the excited expressions on my listeners' faces. I'd then tell of one of the poor heroic characters who was still in the morgue because there was no money to give him a funeral and how the city officials would throw the body in a pine box and bury the person in Potter's Field, with no headboard above the ground for future identification.

I was always sure of hearing these comments from my audience –

"God damn, that was a hell of a thing!"

"Did that really happen?"

"I always heard that New Orleans was a bit of a place."

Then – "Man, give us a drink."

After I had told a few of these tales I would gradually find that everybody knew my name – "Dan this," "Dan that," "Dan, tell so-and-so about that killing," "Dan, is that true about the Hoodoo in New Orleans?"

But most of the time I'd catch the owner watching me out of the corner of his eye, with the expression: I wonder if he knows about that Hoodoo and good luck potions or charms?

While touring with Cab Calloway I carried a large black candle which had burned down to about four inches. It was two inches in diameter. Also three pieces of lodestone which had a hairy fuzzy substance on them. I had a lot of fun with them. I'd leave them in my room on the dresser or table where the landlady or maid could see them. I would place them in front of a small postcard sized photo of St. John the Conqueror. I'd also put a small book called *The Sixth and Seventh Book of Moses* there, until this was stolen. When I left these Voodoo gimmicks about, I knew that when I returned to be lodgings I would have to answer many questions.

With Calloway, I played every town and city of some size in this country and Canada. I cannot recall any place where I, the band boys in Cab's band and other famous bands, had any trouble finding a joint or house of pleasure when we were in the mood for some atmosphere of this sort. We did not go there for the purpose of meeting women, because the women you found there were real wise and most likely beat up. It was mostly for some drinks, some cooked food and laughs, after being on the stage from eleven a.m. to eleven p.m. We did not have to search out women because Cab Calloway's name was magic. "Direct from the Cotton Club in New York City!" – women flocked around the band like bees. A musician's problem was trying to pick out one who appealed to him out of the crowd, most times a dozen deep. You received all sorts of silent signs and messages, smiles, lip talk, even direct proposals. If you had played the place, hall, theatre before, you were in bad shape if you did not know at least some of the women in the crowd of spectators. Many of the cities had noted houses where musicians went after playing. Many of the owners, men and women, were friends of the band, had large collections of the band's records and went to great effort to prepare dinners, suppers and parties for the boys. So when you went to the joints it was mostly for some social action.

Musicians rarely had a problem with the ladies. It was a very monotonous deal sitting on a stage playing one and a half hour stage shows four, five, sometimes six times a day, seven days a week, for months and months at a time. Playing the same songs over and over, under the hot stage lighting. When the stage show was over you went to the small crowded dressing room, always near the roof of the theater. You practiced, worked with your hobby and wrote letters. Many musicians could not take the daily routine, blew their tops and quit. Others waited till after the show and went to a restaurant, cabaret or joint. But in all honesty all these places all over the land were just about the same, with very small differences in set-up. Whisky was available, food and music (juke box, piano) and if you were in the mood, the owner could always call some girls who were not long in appearing.

On one occasion, Calloway's band played a split week in Springfield, Illinois. We arrived in Springfield early in the morning and went right to the theater as was the custom. The musicians and performers brought their instruments and baggage on stage, before departing and scattering all over the Negro section of town to enquire and seek lodgings for the three or four days we were to play there.

From experience, I would ask the stage manager what time the first show was, and what were the interesting places to see in the town. He told me: "Abraham Lincoln's buried here, and it's a must all visitors go to see."

He gave me directions and I went out to the cemetery – Milton Hinton and I, since Milt is a camera bug and has a great collection of pictures. We spent about two hours going out there

127

and talking to the special constable at Lincoln's tomb, as well as reading some of the obituaries on the surrounding tombstones. I find this very soothing to the nerves and peace of mind. You must try that sometime, because it tends to remind you how unimportant a person is in the world, and that the world will go on without you as it went on without you before you came into being.

In skull gardens, you will see majestic mausoleums side by side with humbler ones. It teaches you a lesson that when you have passed and the undertaker folds your hands and your loved ones and friends plant you in the ground, you then become only a memory. No matter how much worldly goods you have accumulated you can't take it with you because shrouds don't have any pockets. Even your dear ones want no part in a graveyard once nightfall comes – when it does, you will lie there a long, long time all alone, by yourself.

When Hinton and I arrived back at the theater, Jonah Jones, Shad Collins, Rudy (Musheed Karweem) Powell and a couple of other musicians were angrily relating an incident to the rest of the troupe. As the story goes, Jonah, Shad, Jeff (Hilton Jefferson), J. C. Heard and Rudy walked into Springfield's largest hotel. When the desk clerk saw them he became very excited, threw up both his hands and yelled, "I'm sorry fellers! But we don't accommodate colored people, and truthfully we are filled up and don't have no rooms!"

The boys stopped, but Rudy, who had become a Moslem, kept walking forward right up to the desk clerk, who was by now surprised. Rudy said, "We are not colored, we are Moslems." Digging into his wallet, he handed the clerk a card.

The clerk said, "You all may be Moslems, but you all look like Negroes to me." Then he read the card carefully, shook his head in a puzzled manner, and observed each member of the group in turn. Finally, he said, "What are you people doing in town?"

Rudy said, "We are passing through and want to stop over for a few days."

The clerk looked at the card again and said, "Well gentlemen, I think I can accommodate you, if you will double up, two to a room."

The group said, "That's okay with us."

The clerk continued, "Gentlemen, I have nothing against colored people, but it is not the custom of the management of this hotel to have Negroes staying here, as our permanent guests would not like it and would move elsewhere."

Rudy said, "Thank you very much, and you can rest assured that we Moslems have nothing whatsoever to do with the American Negro." Then the bellhop took the group to their rooms.

The card Rudy showed the clerk was very impressive. It was stamped with a seal, and there were the crescent, the Star of Arabia, some Arabic words and figures and a Washington D.C. address for the bearer to contact if he got into difficulties.

The topic of conversation back at the theater amongst the troupe was that it was a damned shame how Negro people in America were treated. You could be black as tar, but if you were a foreigner, these simple white folk would accept you. Rudy was a hero, and everybody laughed at how he had conned the desk clerk.

Somebody on the show remarked that if that clerk got suspicious and called the police to investigate, the "Moslems" might end up being sent to jail for misrepresenting themselves. Then Rudy and the "Moslems" got panicky.

Sure enough, somebody connected with the hotel saw the show that afternoon, and told the clerk. He sent word to tell these musicians that they would have to check out of the hotel. The manager of the theater contacted the owner of the hotel and shortly afterwards the band valet went round there and collected all the "Moslem" luggage.

Later on I had Rudy explain to me the set up of the Moslems in the USA. He told me the headquarters were in Newark, N.J., and the leader was a very brilliant man. If you wanted to become a Moslem, you brought this man your application and went to a series of lessons and lectures. When they got through explaining to you what and who you were and traced your background to Africa, you became a new person and your past life was a blank. You lived by the Koran and prayed to Mohammed.

When this smart man had got through washing your brain, even your own mother and father were heathens, according to his doctrine. Rudy had changed his whole family's name. There were dozens of beboppers who joined the sect, and they were an obstinate bunch of cats. One in a well-known band played his home town in the deep South, but he would not even go and see his own mother. He claimed she was not his mother, and he did not remember her or his other relations.

The head of the Moslems in Newark gave you a Moslem name. Lots of these boppers would not answer you if you called them by their former names. One friend of mine, a fine trumpet player, missed lots of work because only his new name was listed in the Local 802 Union directory, and nobody knew who he was.

In Springfield that evening after the second show, I went to a nice café to eat. While I was waiting for the meal, I went to the bar and ordered a bottle of beer. The bartender saw me writing, came over and said, "You a stranger in town?"

I told him I was in the show, and he said, "You look like a newspaper man."

I said, "No, I am writing a jazz book."

He said "Our night cook is an old jazz man from New Orleans."

I said, excitedly, "What is his name?"

"Hamp Benson."

"What time does he come to work?"

"Six o'clock."

That night at seven, after our supper show, I went back over to the café. I sat at the bar and ordered a beer. The bartender served me, and then went into the kitchen, and brought out Hamp Benson to meet me. This is what I wrote down:

Hamp Benson
Interviewed Springfield, Tuesday Dec. 4, 1945

I played the dance at the Pythian Temple Roof Garden with Freddie Keppard's Band the night Jackie Brown, a popular playboy and great dance master, was shot and killed by his sweetheart. A dance master acted as the modern M.C. does, he stood in the center of the dance floor and announced the different routines. While working at the 101 Ranch at Liberty and Bienville,

Tom Anderson offered me a job at one of his clubs, the Arlington Annex. I accepted and taken this group with me:

Hamp Benson – trombone
Arnold Metoyer – cornet
Paul Dominguez – violin
George Thomas – piano (composer of *Hop Scop Blues*)
Henry Martin – drums.

Hamp also talked about Buddy Bolden's band, and remembered Brock Mumford, Willie Cornish, Jimmie Johnson, Frank Lewis and Henry Tillman playing with Bolden. He recalled Bolden playing these jazz classics: *Frog Legs, Palm Leaf Rag, Maple Leaf Rag, Indian Sa Wa, I Thought I Heard Buddy Bolden Say.*

* * *

When I got back to New York, I started thinking about Hamp and what he had had to tell me. The Jazzland Research Guild was the result. The idea was that in my travels around with Cab I'd produce this little questionnaire to give to various people that I met, particularly the older musicians. So I designed this research questionnaire as a way of getting at the truth, as there were a lot of jazz writers starting to write who didn't know all the background. In *A Life In Jazz* I set out details about the "Kids" and the "Kings", Kid Howard, Kid Punch, Kid Rena, King Bolden, King Oliver – all great trumpet players from New Orleans. It's important to remember these names.

I really felt this was true in the 1940s, when the Bunk Johnson band was coming on the scene, and writers were beginning to forget about Kid Ory, Hamp Benson and all the great players of their generation in New Orleans and Chicago. Everything was Jim Robinson, and people did not pay attention to names like Eddie Vinson or George Filhe, who had founded the style, way back.

So I started by sending out about twenty of these questionnaires in the mail, and I got some of them back, from people like Bunk himself, Lionel Tapo, and Adolphe Alexander. Perhaps to start with I got about six or seven, and for a while I was despondent.

I spoke to Sidney Bechet about it. He'd been playing in Boston with Bunk Johnson, and something happened – Bunk got drunk and Sidney fired him, and he sent to New Orleans for Peter Bocage. Meantime Robert Goffin came to visit Bechet, looking like he was the Messiah, and when Goffin was introduced to me he just said "Uh huh." He looked right past me, or through me.

Bechet told me how Goffin had written this great book about jazz. I said, well, if he's so great and he lives over there in Europe, I think I'll write me a book as I'm over here and I'm close to the action.

When I said this, Bechet looked me in the eye and said, "You gotta have *soul* to write a book, you can't just write a book, you know."

He just brushed off what I was talking about as nonsense. So I got back to New York and I decided to persist with the questionnaires. Each one I got back had a different idea about who they thought were important during their time as players, as well as telling about their lives in their own words. My purpose was to ask questions in such a way that one day I could print their answers.

Hamp Benson never did send back the questionnaire, but he wrote me a long letter instead. It stopped very early in his career, but that's what he wanted to tell me, that's the way he was. I'd never met him before we ran into each other in Springfield, but I had heard who he was and what kind of a player. Lee Collins had been spouting on at me about how great Hamp had been, up there with Eddie Vinson who was the best. New Orleans musicians always rate people like this, in terms of a comparison. This is what Hamp wrote:

> I, Hamilton Benson, called Hamp Benson, was born in 1885 at 752 Tchoupitoulas Street, New Orleans, La. My four brothers all played musical instruments. In 1901, I started playing bass. My brother taught me. The first band I played with was a three-piece combination:

Russell Williams, guitar, Johnny Bradley, mandolin, and I played bass. We played in the Red Light District from 1901 to 1903. Johnny Bradley went visiting to Osiko, Miss., and was found dead on the railroad track. That broke up the combination.

After that, in 1903, another combination was made: Jim Williams, violin; Andrew Kimball, cornet; Russell Williams, guitar. We stayed together two years, to 1905. Due to Jim Williams' work as a call boy at the Round House, this combo broke up. A barber, John Hynes on Julius St. near Condolet, had a band named Hill City Band. Andrew Kimball and I joined his four pieces: trombone – John Hynes (manager); Charlie McCurtis [McCurdy] – clarinet; Charlie Pierson – guitar and Cato on drums. The later part of 1906, John Robchaw [Robichaux] had the leading band down there [and] took Kimball from our band. Two months later I joined Tom Brown's band, playing valve trombone which I had been practicing all this time. I also had a slide trombone and the numbers I could play on it I would. Maybe it only be one or two numbers a night, but at last I could play the slide well enough to leave the valve at home. That is the way I started playing the slide.

Tom Brown's band was four pieces and the singer. We played at the Annex on Basin Street. The Annex was the oldest saloon in that district at that time.

I was such a sensation there at the Annex that the manager of the Anderson Cabaret on Rampart and Canal asked me to get six pieces to play at his place. This was my first big band. I got George Thomas, piano; Paul Domingo [Dominguez], violin; Henry Martin, drums; Arnold Matrië [Metoyer], cornet; Peku [Alphonse Picou], clarinet, and I played trombone. We played there until the District closed in 1908.

Then I started booking jobs out of town and used King Oliver, trumpet; Walter Brondon [Brundy], drums; Gabriel, clarinet; George Foster, bass and George Williams, guitar. We had a job playing for the Elks in Slidell, La. After finishing that job, I rented a big ten-room house at 313 Saratoga St. between Pedda and Graber, which I turned into an amusement place where all musicians came after work.

Such people as Bunk Johnson, trumpet; Henry Zeno, drums; George Fields (Filhe), trombone; Peron [Armand J. Piron], violin; Mangle Manedder [Manuel Manetta], piano; Red Happy, drummer; Black Benny, drummer; John Venne [Vigne], drummer; Paul Domingo [Dominguez], violin; Frank Lewis, who was in the oldest jazz band and was Buddy Bolden's clarinet player; Andrew Kimball, cornet; Freddie Keppert [Keppard], cornet; Ernest Dapanuel [Trepagnier]; drummer and many other famous players all came to my house which I kept open for them until 1915.

After 1915 I hit big times.

* * *

Not all the tales of Storyville days came from letters and questionnaires. In the late 1940s, a few years after meeting Hamp Benson, I went back to New Orleans to bury my mother. I remained in town for the following week.

My old friend Joe Robichaux told me that George Baquet was in town. He had bought a bar-room, and his old friend Ernest Trepagnier, who was called "Nenace" by all his New Orleans friends, was manager. Here was an old friendship being revived by two boyhood pals who had not seen each other for at least thirty years. After George had left the Creole band, which had introduced Negro New Orleans jazz to New York City and the many cities on the Orpheum circuit, he had settled in Philadelphia and played and lived there until a doctor advised him that his heart was growing weak. He packed his belongings and returned to New Orleans, where he purchased a bar on the corner of South Rampart Street and Erato. Being careful of his health, he hired Trepagnier as manager and bartender, and he himself took it easy.

Joe Robichaux says, "Son," – my New Orleans nickname is "Son Do" – "Let's go and see Nenace."

So we went uptown to George's bar-room, which was very quiet and empty. There sat George Baquet and Ernest. The place was almost dark, for only a few very small, dim electric bulbs were lit. Ernest recognized Joe at once and we were invited to sit down with them. After a few moments, he also recognized me, for we had worked together in the Alamo Club with Willie Pajeaud's band in 1927.

He introduced me to George, and I reminded him that we had met before in Philadelphia in 1943, when I was there with Calloway's band. Ernest began to laugh as he told George how mischievous I had been on that Alamo job, about all the fun we'd had every night, and all the things that had happened there. He told about Wilhelmina Bart, the pianist, coming to work each night and then promptly falling asleep at eleven p.m., and at times snoring louder than the music of the band.

Also about one time when a guest gave me a drink out of a flask, and the stuff had been so strong that it burned my mouth, so I had to spit it out against the wall, and the paint peeled off that wall. Also about Yank Johnson, the trombonist, who had smeared limburger cheese on my banjo. I put a newspaper soaked with gasoline from my model-T Ford under his chair. When he returned from intermission I lit the paper with a match and burned up his behind. He ran screaming to the bathroom. Some of the white dancing girls felt sorry, as there was lots of smoke on the stand as we stamped out the fire. They wanted the police there to arrest me for attempted murder, but the police laughed because they knew what went on on the bandstand every night.

George Baquet told us that Bou-Boul Fortune (pronounced Fortunay) was the first bandleader to mention and introduce the front line: the Independence Jazz Band's front line consisted of Punkie Valentin, cornet; Bou-Boul Fortune, trombone; and Alphonse Picou, clarinet. Bou-Boul's band was a rival of Bolden. After that, all the bands boasted of their front line; then the fans, second line, promoters and societies boasted about who had the best front line.

Ernest and I sat and drank. Joe did not drink, and nor did George as he was under the doctor's care.

There were many old jazzmen who were mad at Freddie Keppard for not recording with the Creole Band when they were approached by the Victor Recording Company. I asked George why Freddie Keppard had refused to record the Creole Band.

Here is what he told me:

> "The main reason that Keppard did not record during the Creole Band's engagement in New York City at the Winter Garden in 1916 was because of the manner in which he was approached by the officials of the Victor company. Freddie and the other members of the band read the current trade magazines and weeklies. They read *Billboard Advertising* and *Variety*. They knew all about salaries, contracts, the drawing power of various attractions. They knew how many records Caruso sold and what he was paid for those records.
>
> "During intermission one night, the Victor official approached Keppard for the fifth time and handed him a contract to sign. The contract specified that Freddie would receive $25.00 and the sidemen would be paid $15.00 to record four songs. Freddie yelled at the official: 'Take this piece of paper and stick it up your rear. Do I look like a goddam fool? Why, I buy that much whisky a day.'
>
> "The faces of the officials turned scarlet and they scooted out the door. In their haste, they left a copy of the contract which I read. The members of the band angrily shouted as I read out all the long legal clauses that were all in favor of Victor. 'Victor shall have the right to do this. Victor shall have the right to do that.' "

During this time, the Creole Band was the most sensational and exciting attraction on the Orpheum and Pantages circuits. This was the first New Orleans Jazz band to appear publicly in the Northern part of the United States with just six instruments – no piano. Keppard on cornet; Baquet, clarinet; Bill Johnson, bass; Dink Johnson, drums; Eddie Vinson, trombone, and Leon Williams on guitar.

It was always the popular belief that Keppard did not record, for fear his cornet playing would be imitated by others. This is untrue, musicians love to be imitated, for it swells their egos. So, according to George Baquet, the real reason was money and the attitude of the Victor officials. The Creole Band was not poor, they were not stranded and financially they were doing

136

well. Freddie had read about the huge sums of money paid to Caruso for recordings and believed that his music on record would earn something approaching this amount, for he and the Creole Band proved themselves sensations wherever they performed.

I asked George why the band broke up, and he said that other bands started imitating the Creole Band to such an extent that the novelty wore off as far as the public was concerned. Another factor was that the musicians traveled all the time, and Freddie grew tired of this. He was in great demand in Chicago and wanted to settle there.

George said, "The Orpheum Circuit would give us straight thirty or forty weeks' booking, year after year, but they started laying us off after a few years. Then Freddie said we would not have to lay off if we went to Chicago. Dink wanted to settle in California, and I liked Philadelphia. Bill Johnson liked Chicago.

"An agent laid us off in New York City, and Freddie got mad and quit. He said he was going to Chicago to work, and he did so. I went to Philadelphia, Dink left for the West, Leon left for France, Bill left for Chicago. We were all stubborn Creoles, and that was the end of the Creole Band."

Then I asked what it was like when the Navy closed down Storyville – the District.

George said, "I was out on the Orpheum Circuit with the Creole Band."

Ernest and Joe laughed and both went on talking, agreeing that the District was not actually closed down, for the cabarets, bar-rooms and honky-tonks stayed open. Just the landladies and whores moved out to new secret places for the duration of the War. When the war ended, they all moved back to their old haunts.

6
Sit Him Outside On The Steps To Catch Some Fresh Air

This musician's name was Dorsey, fondly called by other musicians, "Li'l Dorsey." I never knew whether Dorsey was his first or last name. He was one of many hundreds of Negro musicians who arrived in New York City's Harlem from cities and towns far and near, who came to the big city in search of fame and fortune. (I was also one of them.)

Dorsey was a drummer, a wonderful drummer. I first saw him playing with Billy Cato's orchestra, a fine band of young, eager, talented musicians. Dorsey was small, just about five feet tall. He was chocolate brown with a perpetual sincere smile molded on his small cherubic face.

One day Jelly Roll Morton looked at Dorsey from a distance and remarked, "What is that boy always grinning about? What's so funny? He ain't got a silver dime in his pocket – and always smiling. He reminds me of the man on the Cream of Wheat box." Jelly's small audience giggled.

This was the month of August in the year 1931 – the height of the Depression. Money was scarce and so was employment. Liquor was prohibited. There were bread lines and food lines, welfare, relief; able-bodied men were selling apples on the street corners. The hit song was, *Brother, Can You Spare a Dime*.

The success of Duke Ellington, Fletcher Henderson, Cab Calloway and McKinney's Cotton Pickers during these hard times encouraged musicians from all over the United States and the many islands of the West Indies to come and try their luck in the Apple – the Big Apple – as New York was called. On the corner of 7th Avenue and 132nd Street stood the Rhythm Club and every newly arrived musician made a beeline for the club. The club was crowded day and night. There you would see all the famous names and noted instrumentalists: Fats Waller, James P. Johnson, Fess Williams, Benny Carter, Coleman Hawkins, Chick Webb, Claude Hopkins and Jelly Roll Morton. In the afternoons in the summer the musicians stopped outside the club and gossiped, formed acquaintances, organized bands and transacted business. On this corner stood the musicians. Across the street stood the underworld characters. Such notorious Harlem figures as Bub Huley, Blue, Shake Snider, Des Verney, Fullback and dozens of other racketeers. In the center of the block on 7th Avenue stood the famous Lafayette Theatre. In front of the theater, on the right side, stood the famous Tree of Hope, right in front of Connie's Inn. Under the tree, the greatest Negro performers congregated in the afternoons to chew the fat and show off their fine clothing. They would pat the old tree, kiss it and make a wish. This was supposed to bring the worshipper extra good luck. This ritual was serious – no joke, no foolishness.

In the afternoons there were these three large clusters of night people:

Jelly Roll would be seen lecturing the musicians.

Bill Robinson would be seen lecturing the performers.

Bub Huley would be seen lecturing the racketeers.

Then Bill Robinson would be seen lecturing any of the three groups. All the performers respected him. The band leaders and musicians respected him. Bill gambled with the racketeers, was a fine pool player and held the world's record for running backwards the sixty yard dash. Another crowd lecturer would be seen, the famous Black Eagle – Colonel Hubert Fauntleroy Julian in his boots and assorted military regalia. It was exciting to see all those famous people daily on the scene.

Down in the large basement under Connie's Inn was the Hoofer's Club – twenty-four hours around the clock you could go down and watch sensational dancing – boys and girls dancing, tapping, trying routines, having cutting contests, dancing to the music of an old upright piano or just hand-clapping or shouting in rhythm.

Three or four weeks on those corners and you had heard and seen the "Who's Who" of Harlem. The men of the underworld gambled in the back rooms of the Rhythm Club; few musicians had gambling money. The racketeers rarely spoke to musicians or male performers. They were cool as they carried a silent contempt for showmen. The ancient adage went: "The cute and pretty little

139

chorus girl ignores the racketeers and their money because she is crazy about the poor sax player."

After a couple of weeks in and about the Rhythm Club, a new arrival would soon join one of the many cliques and syndicates if he could play his instrument fairly well. At the Rhythm Club the two phones were constantly ringing and busy. Ginger, the unofficial manager, himself a well known ragtime piano player, would answer the phones and call out loudly, "Trumpet player wanted!" or "Sax player wanted! Banjo player wanted!" These instrumentalists lined up close to the phone booth and dickered with the caller. If the musician wanted was not on the scene, one of his bunch searched the many neighboring joints for him.

There was a fine trombone player called Geech who was always at the Rhythm Club. He had a wonderful memory of who was called for on the busy phones and would tell you, "Man, you had an important call at such and such a time. I looked all over for you."

Then, with a very sad face he would dramatically, pleadingly, explain to you that he had not eaten since the day or night before. His last morsel of food had gone down his throat forty-eight hours past. He would grimace with stomach pains. He'd plead, "Just let me have a dime please, so I can get a bowl of grits, that's all. Please." Few musicians refused him; you just couldn't. He missed nobody. He could play, would play, but always it was "I don't have a horn," or "I don't have a tuxedo. I don't have a blue suit. I don't have a white shirt."

Many musicians helped him get these things – then it was the same tale of woe again. He finally got enough dimes and quarters and promptly disappeared. We never saw him again.

On different afternoons you could go near the Tree of Hope and see just about any of the big name stars in colored show business. This was Harlem, New York City – The Big Apple. These show folks would congregate there with their show face smiles and personalities, shaking hands, back patting, acting like they had not see one another in years. There would be much ogling, looking one another over from head to foot, much gossiping, signifying – everybody all smiles. They came to show off their fine clothes, both men and women. This was exciting to me, for I had just arrived from New Orleans where the Depression was raising havoc. I had three outdated suits and here I saw many of the men performers dressed in different outfits every day. I would hear many of the performers say, "I'm going home to change these clothes," and they'd reappear an hour later all togged up in another complete outfit. These performers were all big time and looked happy and prosperous. Of course, there were many who looked depressed. They would be chatting happily, however. On other afternoons you would see Mamie Smith, Clara Smith, Bessie Smith, Trixie Smith, Lucille Hegamin, Ethel Waters, Nina Mae McKinney, Dancing Dotson, Early "Snakehips" Tucker.

Freddie "Snakehips" Taylor would drive up and park his Cord automobile which was, at that time, rare and modernistic. Freddie was a handsome young man – immaculate – real good looking, soft spoken and friendly. Everybody liked him, both men and women. His brand new Cord automobile would attract more people – they would gape at the car and then Freddie, as he and friends sat in the shining new Cord, chatting. Besides the famous Smith girls there were other Smith singers: Mary Smith, Louise Smith, Grace Smith, Gladys Smith, Pearl Smith. I would see all these women but did not meet them until later in some small night club or other. They would be announced, "Miss so-and-so Smith will now sing." Later, patrons would ask, "Are you Mamie's sister or Bessie's Sister?" The dry retort was "Oh no, we are no kin," or "She's a distant relation of mine." I met and played for many a singer with the name of Smith.

Under the Tree you would often hear, "I just got in from England, France, Spain, Germany. I'm leaving next week for Spain, Italy, Belgium." You'd see the Berry Brothers, Step Brothers, Four Flash Devils, Palmer Brothers, Five Cracker Jacks, Wells, Mordecai and Taylor, Moss and Frye. If they were in town for a while they made the scene. It was the same with the musicians and I am sure with the racketeers, "I just left Sing Sing, Dannemora, Riker's Island, The Tombs," or "I was convicted, my trial comes up on the fifteenth, I'm out on bail." There would also be great handshaking amongst the racketeers, some newly arrived thug from Buffalo, Pittsburgh, or Chicago being given the welcome mat.

Another group on the scene whom I saw and met were about fifteen little hunch-backed men who gathered with the three groups. There was the famous Chick Webb with the musicians, Money with the racketeers and Joyner with the performers. Joyner was a great performer, Money a noted gambler, Chick Webb the great drummer and there were these others – all hunchbacked. They were not beggers and did not seem burdened by their affliction. They were all neat and talented in their chosen professions. It was strange to see all those little crippled men carry on.

On the corner one afternoon I was listening to one of Jelly Roll's famous lectures. These were very enlightening. One of the musicians standing in the crowd around Jelly grunted, "Oh, oh, there's Jack the Bull!" and the crowd looked across the street to see Jack the Bull getting out of a police cruising car.

"All right!" he yelled, "I'll take this corner!" He was addressing the racketeers on the opposite corner.

I had seen the Bull a few times before. Once he had yelled "All right, I'll take this corner!" and the three groups had suddenly dispersed, walking off in all directions. Another time he had yelled from a distance up the street and thrown his night stick real hard and I had been amazed as I watched the stick bounce end over end as the large cluster of night folks dispersed. It was the Bull's duty to disperse crowds and these crowds of night people would get awfully large. On some afternoons all these celebrities standing about would attract many passers-by.

On this particular afternoon, when Jack the Bull yelled, "I'll take this corner!" the racketeers did not seem to be in a hurry to move on. Standing over there were Bub, Blue and hunchbacked Money. The Bull stepped upon the sidewalk and yelled with authority, "I say, I'll take this corner."

Then the men did begin to move, but very slowly. Angrily the Bull yelled, "What's wrong with you?"

Fullback, standing alone, folded his thick arms and growled, "I don't feel like moving."

The crowd stood off as the Bull reared back on his haunches with his chest raised. He and Fullback faced each other.

Jelly Roll, who had stopped talking, was watching the scene and said cautiously, "Oh, Oh – this is it. The lion done met the tiger."

Groups on both corners watched as the racketeer Fullback defied the tough copper, Jack the Bull. When I had seen Fullback swaggering about the club, the corners, and the Tree of Hope, I had wondered about his monniker, "Fullback" – a name associated with football, college. He was a big healthy looking guy, six feet tall and about two hundred pounds – healthy – all muscle. But his manner and nasty, filthy talk did not suggest that he had ever passed through a college gate. We all looked on as Jack the Bull shouted, "I said get off this corner."

Fullback yelled back, angrily, "You're bad because you got that uniform, that club, that pistol, that billy. If you take off them pistols and that billy, I'll whip you off this corner."

The large crowd became tense as Jack the Bull replied, "O.K. Fullback, you been asking for it and I'm gonna give you your wish."

The Bull unbuttoned his coat, took it off and handed it to the white policeman who had now stepped out of the police car. He handed him his gun, club, billy, cap, tie and wrist watch. At the same time, Fullback was taking off his things, placing them on the sidewalk (for he stood alone; all his racketeer buddies were cautiously keeping their distance.) Then the Bull yelled, "You ready?" and Fullback yelled back, "You're damn right!"

The two big men squared off like two professional fighters. They shuffled about for a while and Fullback punched the Bull on the jaw with a roundhouse right. The Bull was furious as the large crowd yelled and groaned, "Ahhhhhhhhhhhh! Ohhhhhhh!"

The Bull feinted with his right hand and his left was swiftly buried in Fullback's fat healthy belly – he grunted and bent over. The Bull struck him a terrific blow beside the head and Fullback toppled over, his round head striking the hard, rough concrete pavement. He fell stretched out and quivered, his whole body in a sort of spasm, then he stretched out like he was in bed. The huge crowd was silent except for a few hurrahs which diminished with the hard cold stares of the onlookers. The Bull, who was winded and out of breath, smiled as the white cop patted him on his back. The Bull was still angry as he began to put back his weapons while looking down at the prostrate Fullback.

A storekeeper rushed out of his shop carrying a large bucket of water. The Bull slowly poured the water on Fullback's head and face. He awakened, slowly sat up and looked about, dizzily. He shook his head and felt the side of his face which was swollen, bloody and bruised from his fall to the sidewalk. He looked up from the two feet that stood in front of him to the blue pants, then to the knees, waist, chest and into the face of the scowling Jack the Bull. He shook his head and looked all about, trying to grasp what had happened. The Bull yelled, "Get up, Fullback!"

He tried, but couldn't. A couple of his racketeer friends looked sheepish as they came over and lifted him to his feet and helped him on with his coat and his high, light gray, Stetson hat.

The Bull yelled, "Get in the car. You're going to jail!" and the other cop opened the door of the police car. Fullback stepped off the sidewalk and slowly got into the car. The Bull turned to the large group that had gathered and stood a good distance off and shouted at them, "I'll take this corner!" Everyone started to move as the Bull got into the car and it drove off slowly. When the police car was out of sight, the crowd again gathered at the corner to discuss the brawl.

Jelly Roll said, laughingly, "You all think Fullback got a whipping – wait till the Bull gets him in the precinct! That was an idiotic thing to do – challenge an officer of the law. Fullback can't whip Jack the Bull. Police stay in physical condition. They exercise every day. Fullback is fat, eating all the ham hocks and greens. He don't exercise; he smokes cigarettes and reefers."

Everyone laughed. Jelly continued, "He drinks that bad rot gut whisky, stays up all night. Them reefers told him to challenge the Bull." The crowd went hysterical.

The next day Fullback was on the scene, talking to the racketeers. The right side of his face was bandaged but other than that he was the same, still walking and talking with his usual notorious swagger. The gossips said that Jack the Bull took Fullback to the Harlem Hospital and had him doctored up, then to the precinct. Fullback was placed on bail, charged with assault on a police officer. The Bull did not press charges. Jelly remarked,

"They gonna squash the case."

A few weeks later, in October, when the crowds on the corner had become much smaller because of the breezy weather, the Bull came on the scene. He said nothing as he passed the dozen or so racketeers. He crossed the street and said nothing as he passed the group of musicians and continued to walk briskly down towards the Tree of Hope. He only yelled when the crowds were too thick.

On the long block on 132nd Street where the Rhythm Club stood, there were long rows of brownstone houses lining both sides of the street. These were six-storied buildings which all looked alike. As they were all of identical construction, a newcomer had to remember his house number or he could easily enter the wrong house. Simon Marrero, the great New Orleans bass player, looked down at the long row of houses and remarked, "Hot damn; all them houses look just like hospitals! That ain't living, all them people stacked up, piled up, living on top of one another, living like rats!"

The houses had originally been residences of well-to-do early white New Yorkers, but with the Southern Negro migrating in, the whites had departed and the new tenants rented rooms in these brownstones, which became tenements. Every brownstone had a large basement which was also divided into rooms and rented. In the basements of this long block there must have been a half-dozen speakeasies running full-blast twenty-four hours around the clock. During the day and night the musicians who drank would slowly walk from the Rhythm Club in small groups along the long block and they would suddenly disappear down the steps into one of the "speaks." I made many trips down this block. All these speaks were named after their owner, Rufus, Memphis, Georgia Boy, Charleston or Possum.

When you entered a speak it was just like going into a large Southern kitchen. There was the smell of Southern delicacies: pigs' feet, collard and mustard greens and the strong odor of stale alcohol. Most of the toilets were ancient, ugly and noisy. There was always an old feeble or lazy cat or dog sleeping right in the pathway. All of these places were dimly lit and when your eyes became adjusted to this atmosphere you could make out the eerie figures of men and women sitting motionless in the dark corners. Not one muscle would move as they looked at you through half-closed eyes. They would never return a smile but would just stare at you, these ghostly characters, sitting still as death. But around the large center tables, which were usually covered with oil cloth which was marked with a million cigarette burns, there sat the live ones, as the spenders were called. At these tables you heard all sorts of fantastic spine-tingling stories. What story tellers!

Once they got started, each tale was more potent than the one before. You soon forgot the zombies in the corner, then suddenly one would take on a violent coughing spasm, chronic deathly coughs, wheezing, hocking, choking, spitting, heavy breathing. The silence, broken by the proprietor's commanding yell, "Man (or woman), nigguh, bitch, sonofabitch, half-dead bastard, get up and get in that toilet, in the shit house and puke up that stuff."

Then the slow-moving cougher would stagger off to the toilet. Then more insults: "That so-and-so is dying on his feet. Taking medicine and drinking whisky. Don't eat, just drinks. Whisky, no food."

Generally, the tale-telling would stop, everybody annoyed by the coughing. Most times, when the cougher would come out of the toilet, the owner, Rufus, or Possum, or whoever, would walk towards the slow-moving cougher and lead him to the door, yelling, "You half-dead bitch (or bastard) get out of here, and keep your drunken no-good black ass out of here."

Then there would be this soft knocking and pleading from the outside: "Please let me in. I'm all right."

Then the nasty reply, "Sonofabitch get away from that door!"

The owners of these booze dungeons all had the same sort of personality and all seemed to share a cold attitude towards life; they were surprised at nothing they heard, even the most drastic calamities. "So what! That's life!" was their typical reaction. Seems like they would frequent the other joints and then decide to open themselves a dungeon. There was the Depression going on, no work around and most of the furnishings in these spots were ancient, threadbare, broken, greasy and nothing matched. There would be three or four sofas, the arms of which were discolored from the grease of thousands of hands.

A few of these men had wives with the same worldly attitudes. Nothing impressed them. They were all of the same breed. You would frequent one of these joints and over a period of months a half dozen sweethearts of the owner would appear. Taking charge, cooking, cleaning, selling booze and they'd soon vanish, to be replaced by another.

"Where's Flossie?" you would ask.

Memphis would snarl, "That no good bitch? I got rid of her. I put that whore out!" or "She was an alcoholic."

Oh, there were hundreds of other nasty answers.

Each of the joints was a miniature social club and if you were well behaved and could sit or stand up under the daily drinking of the "smoke", and would pay your tabs punctually, you were welcome. There were also regular speakeasies, many of them, but they served bottled bootleg whisky by the shot glass and this was expensive in time of Depression. Yes, money was scarce and the price of a drink in a speakeasy would buy a pint of smoke in a joint. Once you became addicted to the taste of smoke you formed a dislike for branded whisky. I saw many a smoke drinker refuse a drink of bonded whisky.

All the owners of the smoke joints would go into tantrums defending the quality, purity and potency of their smoke.

You could play your numbers there as the numbers runners included these smoke joints in their rounds. When the number men came in at all hours they would ask you what number you liked. The scene at these times would always be very humorous, for you would hear all this kind of talk:

> "I had a dream"
> "What you dreamt?"
> "I dreamed I was a white man."
> "Oh, a white man is 416."
> "Gimme that for a dime."
> Another would say, "Gimme 300 for a quarter."
> "Oh, that's the dog number. Did you dream about a
>   dog?"
> "No, my dog died."

The Harlem shops sold a dozen varieties of number and policy books. These are small dictionaries and they read like this:

Dog	300
Cat	200
Mule	211
Cottonfield	060
Coffin	111
Dead man	201
Dead woman	309
Black woman	000
Black man	001
White man	416
Police	880
Fireman	910
Fire	911

Arguments would start about the right number for the right subject.

"Ah dreamed there was a fire and a white man ran out of the house naked – then a black man ran out, he was barefooted, dressed in long red underwear. The police and the fire engines arrived just in time to catch a jet black woman in a white night gown who jumped out of a five story window down in the fireman's net."

"A fireman is 910."

"White man is 416."

"Black woman is 300."

"Black man is 301."

"Red pajamas is 444."

"Fire engine is 841."

"Five stories is 555."

"Fire is 119."

"If there was a fire there must have been smoke – that's 550."

"I didn't see no smoke."

"Well, Goddamn, who ever seen a fire without smoke!"

"I didn't see no smoke – next you gonna say I see ashes."

This would continue until the number runner announced, "I gotta leave." Then, one, two or all the numbers were played from a penny a number to a quarter.

When these runners would sell you a number, there wasn't a ticket, they marked down your number with your name or your nickname by it. And if you hit, you got around eight dollars for a nickel. The draw was from the racetrack. It was above reproach. You couldn't question that. At 2 o'clock after the first race, that was the first number. 3 o'clock, or the fifth race, or something similar, would be the second number, and the eighth race was the third number. So there was time for this guy to go all around for each race. You'd hear:

"What number do you want on the first race?"

"Gimme a dollar on the two!"

Around 4 p.m. the last number would come out and be relayed by word of mouth, "811 is the figure." You could hear, "That's Sam's number!" or "That's Jake's number!" or "That's Bub's number; that's his number – he's kept that number for years – you can bet your black ass he's got it," and if the winner was a customer in the joint, you would get stoned out of your head that evening because the winner would come by as soon as he got paid his winnings and he would treat everybody.

The concoction served in these joints was called "smoke" because it was white but cloudy. It was served in a small mug, which crockery was originally used as a milk container. The end was shaped like a cow's head and the liquor was poured through the cow's open mouth. A handle was formed by the cow's tail. This mug was the standard measurement used in all the joints. No matter how long the liquor stood in the glasses it remained cloudy in color; it never cleared. Two or three drinks of smoke numbed your senses, dimmed your sight, burned your throat and chest, set your belly on fire and slowed your every movement. A half dozen drinks would put you into a trance. Your tongue became heavy and your jaws worked slowly.

Smoke was delivered in clear white, gallon jugs. I spent many hours in these dungeons but not once did I witness a smoke delivery. I've often wondered about that. The smoke would be poured from the gallon jugs into quart bottles and then into the cow shaped mugs. When a customer ordered a cow mug of smoke

149

(which would cost either fifteen, twenty or twenty-five cents,) the owner asked, "How many glasses?"

Some characters would growl, "One".

Others ordered four or five. The mug held about six whisky glasses and you were never obliged to buy another customer a drink. I'd see customers come in completely sober, order a mug of smoke and in twenty minutes become completely drunk, helpless and idiotic. After drinking the smoke I would gradually start giving off gas – from my top and bottom. I'd get shortwinded and my nostrils would give off a wheeze. My stomach would growl, grumble and become restless. I love story telling and in these joints you merely had to mention a subject or a problem and the drama unfolded. As the customers talked, argued and debated someone would sneakily and silently give off gas. Occasionally a customer would do so with musical sounds which would be followed by laughter or funny comments. If the owner was in a bad mood the offender was asked to clear out, "Git outside and let the breeze blow on ya."

If the odor was not accompanied by a sound there would be a mystery but nobody would admit their guilt. "Not me!" everyone would claim.

Coming from New Orleans, the new scene was very fascinating to me. In these joints you could be enlightened on any subject. Just start asking some questions or act deeply concerned about some problem and you would get all sorts of solutions. Sitting about there would be a disbarred layer and another who could never pass the state bar although he had taken the exams fifteen times. There might be others present who had finally "took to booze." Many of these dungeons were operated by women. You would hear:

> "Alberta died." –
> "What Alberta?"
> "Alberta that's got the joint."
> "Fool, I know six or seven Albertas that's got joints. There's Yellow Alberta on 136th Street, Skinny Alberta on Lenox Avenue. There's merriney Alberta next to the Savoy on 140th Street and the bull-dyking 'Berta on Seventh Avenue. If I get to thinking I can call a dozen

Albertas – so when you say Alberta explain which of
them no good bitches you talking 'bout.   Alberta,
Alberta, Alberta and there's old white whisky headed
Alberta from Texas, stays with Black Sam."

Drinking smoke was very popular with the smoke dungeon cree-
pers. It was a challenge to the youngsters to drink it down "like a
man" and keep a straight face. The old timers would generally
watch the facial expressions of a drinker as he swallowed his
drink. Without realizing it the onlookers would mimick the expression of the drinker, using their lips and lower facial muscles.
This drink would leave a variety of tastes in your mouth and on
your tongue. As you sat at a table, talking or listening, your tongue
would taste flashes of fiery hot pepper, lemon, garlic, alcohol,
corn, or molasses, and your nostrils too would get flashes of the
odors of chicken, paint, pickles and many foul odors. To stop this
annoyance, one would gulp another drink of smoke. This seemed
to dull the taste and smell for awhile. Not too long ago I read an
article concerning bootleg liquor. This article cleared up the mystery of all those nasty tastes and smells for it stated that the bootleggers would throw any and all sorts of decayed animal matter
into their vats of fermenting mash: rotten chickens, vegetables,
chicken guts. Also many insects: roaches, gnats, bedbugs, spiders,
lice, as well as rats and mice. Enough of that!

These bootleggers stocked their stills in top apartments,
leaving the windows open so that the strong fumes could ev-
aporate and not descend into the lower apartments. It is likely
that a few bats swiftly flew inside the open windows to fall into
the open mash vats.

When a job was available for a musician the word spread
quickly at the Rhythm Club. If the instrumentalist was not about
one of the many stooges who hung around would go off and
search all the joints – Rufus, Possum, Charleston. There was this
clique of musicians who spent all their waking moments at the
Rhythm Club or down in one of the many smoke joints. Some
musician in the club would yell to the stooge, "Go down to 212"
(or 230 or 218 or 224). To know which of these identically
constructed buildings was meant, a good memory was necessary.

151

One had to remember some mark or identification on the front of the place; a curtain at the window or a damaged spot on the stairway or else a person could knock on one iron gate, thinking it was another and be met with an annoyed voice, shouting "Possum's place is at 228."

Big Green, Fletcher Henderson's great trombone player, was a bitter man and the smoke had begun to show its effect on his large body. He was a sorry sight to see for he had lost weight and his expensive clothes hung on him as if he was a scarecrow. After he left Fletcher's great band, few leaders would hire him. Daily he and a dozen or so other drinking musicians could be seen in a huddle as they made a pool of their money to buy smoke in one of the joints.

As Green and his bunch of boozers slowly walked to a smoke joint, the sober musicians who saw him would shake their heads with pity and remark, "What a shame, such a great musician going to the dogs."

I noted that smiling Li'l Dorsey had joined Big Green's many daily parades. Sometimes one of Green's gang was missing and soon you would hear, "So-and-So is in the Harlem Hospital." However, Big Green would lead his remaining group down the street.

I visited one of the other joints one afternoon. As soon as my eyes had become adjusted I made out the figure of Li'l Dorsey. He seemed transfixed as he sat there in the zombie stillness. His eyes were half-open but the smile was gone from his little round face. I realized that it had been some time since I had seen that big, kind smile of his around the Rhythm Club. Nowadays when I did see him it would be occasionally, and then from a distance, as he staggered out of one basement and across the street into another one.

Now the musicians who followed Big Green on his trips into the smoke joints were all considered fine musicians. If they were not, I'm not sure he would have tolerated their company. Green was bitter and angry at the world. After he left Fletcher's orchestra, which was then recognized as the greatest in the world, playing in all those other bands was a step down the musical ladder for him. Also a step down in prestige as well as finances.

Musicians who joined Green's group were aloof as far as the other groups of musicians were concerned. They stood apart, in huddles, straight-faced and rarely smiling. They would discuss the social and economic conditions. When Green was greeted he returned a gruff, "Yeah, yeah, hello," but never with a smile.

Li'l Dorsey had reason for following Green and taking to booze. He couldn't recall deliberately offending anyone; he could play and would play; he was punctual; he was neat – he just couldn't understand what was happening –he was fired from every job. Big Green and the bunch understood Dorsey's problem and I'm sure told him: "Man, them dirty so-and-so's are jealous of you. That's all it is. They are jealous 'cause you can play; you sell what you play and all the women crowd round you. That's it, they are jealous. Them cats grin in your face, then stab you in the back."

So Li'l Dorsey began to see the light. Jealousy! Dorsey's personality projected, his sincere smile was electric; you just had to watch him for he played with the constant toothy smile so familiar to us all, and the jazz lovers would crowd around in front of the stand. "What's he gonna do next?"

He had watched all the great New York City drummers and added their best tricks to his many eye-catching gimmicks. He loved those drums and knew the rudiments. He had mastered:

> Baby Dodds' shimmy-shuffle,
> George Stafford's driving press roll,
> Kaiser Marshall's dynamic cymbal breaks,
> Chick Webb's sudden explosions,
> Cuba Austin's scene stealing tricks,
> Walter Johnson's smooth perfection,
> Paul Barbarin's New Orleans beat.

Band vocalists were annoyed at Dorsey, for when he sang his few hot fast numbers he received more applause than they did. Waiters were not too fond of him either because of the constant questions directed at them: "Who is that drummer?", "What's his name?"

The owners' girl friends were attracted to him: "That drummer is so cute", "I love to watch that drummer".

A bandleader fired him when he heard a group of women admirers suggest to Dorsey, "Why don't you get your own band? You are the whole band. Without you they are nothing. I came here to see you. You are wasting your time with this band."

Then one afternoon, outside the Rhythm Club, a group were engaged in serious conversation. I heard one say, "It's a damn shame, poor boy. A great drummer: that smoke killed him."

Here are the details of Dorsey's passing: Li'l Dorsey died while seated on a chair in the dark corner of one of the smoke dungeons. There was nothing unusual about a well behaved customer sitting in a chair in a dark corner. He could stay as long as he pleased, all day and all night, for the joints never closed and were rarely without drinking customers. Many a patron just sat there when he couldn't manage to pay his room rent. Li'l Dorsey would sit for hours in the joints. He was never any bother; he never begged for drinks. On one particular morning a lively customer said to the owner, "Give Dorsey a drink!" and a drink was poured and taken over to Dorsey.

"Here's your drink, Dorsey" said the owner. There was no reply. The man shook Dorsey. Dorsey did not move. He shook him again. Dorsey did not budge. He put the drink down and shook Dorsey violently. He lit a match and opened one of Dorsey's eyes. Then he felt Dorsey's head, hands, temple. He was frightened.

"This man is acting dam' peculiar over here" he said. Then he began to yell, "You all come over here and see if y'all kin do sumpin' with him."

The other patrons lit matches. They noted a pool of water on the floor and noted too that the side of Dorsey's trouser leg was wet. Finally two men picked up the chair with Dorsey in it and brought him to the lighted portion of the room. There was a strange silence as one of the men began to examine Dorsey. He pinched him and shook him. Then he called for a mirror which was placed close to Dorsey's nose, but it showed no moisture. The men tried to lift the body which had become stiff; the arms and legs would not move freely. He announced, "This man is dead."

"Are you sure he's dead?" the owner asked, fearfully.

"Dead as a door knob" was the reply.

The owner gasped, "I'll be a sonofabitch; a dead man in

here! Now I'm in trouble."

"What you gonna tell the police?"

"How can I explain this shit?"

"What time is it?"

"It's four thirty."

The owner hurried out the door. As soon as he was gone one man got the gallon jug of smoke which was in the corner and each man in the group had a large drink. Then they had another. When the owner returned he was trembling. "We gotta get him outa here and fast!" he stated in a scared voice.

They all looked at Dorsey who sat stiffly in a chair. His right elbow rested on his knee and his chin was cupped in his open hand. It seemed a comfortable, snoozing position. The men drank and looked at Dorsey. One man went out front as a lookout. The owner and another patron lifted Dorsey out of the chair. (His stiff little body remained in the rigid, sitting position.) As they lifted him both men groaned, "God damn, this body is heavy."

The lookout grunted, "Come on, all's clear."

It was five a.m. and the street was dark, deserted and quite still. They quickly walked up the few steps to the sidewalk, crossed the street and stopped at a brownstone which was about four buildings away, where they hurriedly deposited Dorsey's body on the stoop in his stiff sitting position. Then they scampered back down to the joint. The lookout came in smiling. He said, "He's sitting on them steps just like he was sitting in here. He looks like he's catching some fresh air."

The owner wasn't amused, "I hope nobody seen us take him out of here. Drink up," he said. "I'm closing up."

And that's what they did. The owner put out the light and locked the door and they all quickly walked to Lenox Avenue where they scattered.

Now it was seven a.m. and hundreds of people in the neighborhood awoke and began to stir about. Folks came out of the brownstones. People were going to work, children were going to school. Soon it was eight o'clock. There sat Dorsey; nobody paid a bit of attention to him. Just another drunk sleeping it off. A very common sight.

The madam of the brownstone, as was her customary

155

habit, came out of her first floor apartment carrying a broom. She started to sweep the long hall; she swept the wine bottles and other accumulated rubbish out of the door and down the steps, all over Dorsey. When she saw him she shouted, "You bum! Get the hell off'n these steps. You drunkard fool. Where the hell you think you at? At your house? You hear me? Git off'n these steps."

Folks passing by stopped and looked on as she continued to yell. Finally she struck Dorsey across his back with the broom. Dorsey keeled over and fell to the sidewalk in his stiff seated position. He did not move. There was a wet spot where Dorsey sat. The woman stood there, gripping the broom handle with her eyes popping and her mouth wide open. She whispered, "That's funny. He's not moving."

People began to gather. "What's going' on? What happened?"

One of the many police cars that prowl the streets of Harlem slowly drove up and stopped. The cop took his time about getting out of the green car and pushing his way through the large crowd that had congregated as he called, "All right, open up, get back, move!"

He looks, stoops and jabs Dorsey with his night stick and asks the woman who is still clutching her broom, "D'ya live here?"

In a small voice she replies, "Yes, officer."

He asks, "You got a phone?"

"Yes" she answers, in that same small voice.

He tells her, "Call the Harlem Hospital for an ambulance!" and she hurries inside.

"Move on!" the policeman yells to the crowd. The ambulance finally arrives. The men in the white coats examine Dorsey. The body is lifted on a stretcher and placed inside the ambulance. The ambulance leaves. The policeman is busy with pencil and paper as he questions the woman. The crowd disperses. When the policeman has finished with the frightened woman the wet spot where Dorsey sat is barely visible.

The musicians on the corner all wore long sorry expressions as many versions of the story were related. Then came the questions: "Where's the body?"

"Where's his home town?"

"Who's his kinfolks?"

"Is his union dues paid up?"

"Where was he rooming at?"

"Does Big Green know?"

I listened to the musicians and their many comments. For about a week Li'l Dorsey's tragic passing was the main topic on the corner. I never heard of a funeral for Li'l Dorsey or any real true details of what happened to his remains.

I was sitting in Charleston's smoke dungeon a few months later. There, seated in the corner in that stiff, still, zombie position was Big Green. His eyes were open: he was cross eyed, one eye was focused on the ceiling and the other on the floor.

Charleston noticed that I was looking at Big Green. He laughed and yelled nastily, "Green, git your ass out'n dat corner befo' you sit up there and die like the drummer did."

Green did not budge. His eyes just opened wide, then slowly closed. Somebody asked, "What drummer died?"

Charleston laughed. Then frowning, he said, "That li'l drummer Dorsey died, sitting in a chair in that dirty son of a bitch Possum's joint across the street. Them dirty bastards waited until four o'clock in the morning when it was dark and the street was clear. They toted the corpse just like it wuz sitting in the chair and they sat it on that big mouth inquisitive bitch Bessie Morgan's steps. Serves the bitch right; she came out sweeping, hit the corpse with the broom: just like a old witch, the bitch. The corpse keeled over, the dirty-assed police came, the ambulance came, took the corpse to the morgue. The old nosey bitch was shocked shitless, the shock was so drastic she took sick; she's been in bed every since. Now we can have some peace on this block. Serves the old bitch right."

He paused and yelled, "Git up, Green, and see: you might wanna pee."

Big Green's eyes slowly opened and slowly closed.

I looked over at Big Green who was seated in the warm, dark corner with the other still and silent smoke addicts. They all wore some sort of overcoat. This was October and it was cold; the Rhythm Club corner was not as crowded on these nippy afternoons as it had been during the summer. The leaves had fallen from the Tree of Hope. The performers and the racketeers were all indoors. The winter breezes left the smoke houses packed and busy. If the weather was very cold the characters would hurry inside, rubbing their cold hands and shouting, "Hawkins is out there looking for every living thing." Then there was this great winter hibernation.

As I said, these were Depression days and there was no work for these poor people. Everybody sort of shared with one another. On the stoves in these joints were big pots containing rice, chicken, all parts of the hog, greens and cornbread. This was for the evening meal and the food was sold by the plateful for a pittance or just given away to the regulars. There was a certain character who always came in with a case of cold storage chicken and other foods. He was always in a hurry and would shout, "Don't ask where I got it; do you want to buy it?" It was bought.

As I said the characters stayed indoors. Unless, of course, they had urgent business or if they were chased, in which case they would just go to another dungeon. No more fresh air until the spring. The windows were barred and the holes were stopped up. When the door opened a nasty chorus of shouts began, "Close dat goddamn door!"

It was very quiet. The dozen or so customers were in deep meditation and I said to Charleston, "Who's the greatest trombone player in the world?"

Charleston seemed surprised. "Are you kidding," he replied. "There he is, sitting over there in the corner, the drunken simple bastard!"

One of the men joined the conversation, "I don't know about that. What about Jimmy Harrison?"

Green didn't move a muscle. Charleston said, "I'm gonna tell you what I saw with my own two eyes and what I heard with my own two ears. When this big, cross-eyed bum feels like playing with Henderson's band at the Roseland he came into the Band Box just at the time when about ten of the greatest trombone players were having a cutting contest. You never heard such blowing in all your life. They saw Green when he came in and what blowing! I'm telling you it was a bitch. Well, Green stood at the bar drinking a big water glass full of gin. Somebody hollered,

'Come on, Green – play your horn!'

"Green ignored the hollering. Then Kaiser Marshall grab-bed up one of the trombones and handed it to Green. Green took the horn and held it as he swallowed a full glass full of gin. He just looked at all of them, each of them a hell of a trombone player. Someone yelled, 'Big Green is skeered.' That did it!

"Green slowly walked to the center of the floor and looked at them cats with his cross-eyes. One eye was looking at heaven and the other was peering deep down in hell.

"I'll never forget this until my dying day and the good Lord up in heaven is my secret judge. Green said one word to the piano player 'B flat'. Then he played *My Buddy* in waltz time: three choruses of *My Buddy*. Hot damn he played! The waltz was so pretty and so sweet that it made tears come to your eyes.

"After the way Green played *My Buddy*, in waltz time, he took every ass by surprise. He's a slick bastard. Then you know what happened? All them hell of a trombone players, and they was all masters, they slowly and nicely put all the trombones in the cases where they belonged, especially when the master, Big Green, is around. And who was there that night (God bless the dead) playing the trap drum? It was that same Li'l Dorsey who this character (at this point Charleston pointed to an elderly man sitting at the table) helped carry with Possum and sat on the stoop."

The man did not reply nor change his expression. Everybody looked at him as Charleston pointed and then began to shout accusingly, "This old bastard, son of a bitch, was in cahoots with the whole thing. He helped Possum carry the corpse and sit it on the steps. Then he went up to his room at 344 and sat up in his window peeping at the whole scene. But his conscience started whipping him and he could not sleep. So he just sat at the window, peeping down from behind the curtain from 5 to 9 a.m. until the ambulance done drove the corpse to the morgue."

Charleston finished his speech by snarling at the man, "You low-lifed dog."

The man said, in defense, "Possum just said 'let's just sit him outside to catch some fresh air."

The man bowed his had and spoke very earnestly, "We did

159

what we thought was right; we saw that the boy was dead and if we called the police we would have had to give account of how he died; we would have had to go to jail and do a whole lot of explaining to the police. We would have had to get lawyers and none of us ain't got no money.

"The boy wasn't killed in that place. He just died. His heart gave out on him. Whose fault was that? Putting the body on the steps outside was no crime. The boy was dead; there was no life in the body. Had he showed life I would have taken him to the Harlem Hospital like I done many times before. I don't have no guilty conscience. Possum and everybody that hanged in the joint liked that boy. He wasn't eating, just drinking smoke. He didn't have no room so Possum just let him sleep on the chair in the corner. I felt sorry for the boy because he was in bad shape. He hadn't taken his shoes off for days and his ankles were swollen. He just drank himself to death, didn't care about living any more. I can take you to a dozen smoke joints and show you dozens of men and women sitting around with swollen ankles doing just what Li'l Dorsey did, committing suicide. The police know what's happening: cases like Dorsey's happen every day. He's just one of them people who lose the will to live, cowards."

Somebody called out, "How could the body sit up without falling?"

Charleston answered, "Damn fool! *Rigor mortis* had set in the corpse. Don't you know when a person dies as soon as his blood gets cold *rigor mortis* takes over and the body gets stiff? It stays in whatever position its in; sitting, squatting, kneeling, praying. Whatever position the breath leaves your body in, that's the position you stay in."

I asked, "How did they straighten the body out?"

Charleston glanced at me and shook his head in disgust. He yelled, "Idiot! The undertaker uses a hammer, a hatchet, an axe or a saw and breaks the corpse's bones. Then he sets them in the right relaxed position. You don't think the undertaker would lay out a corpse in a sitting position, do you? Did you ever see a corpse in a sitting or kneeling position? If you did, run here and get me so I can see this too and then I will kiss your behind on Broadway at five o'clock in the evening in front of the Palace

Theatre; and you know it's crowded at five in the afternoon."

He looked at me quizzically and asked, "You from New Orleans?"

"Yes," I said.

"How long you been in New York?" he wanted to know.

"Three months" I answered.

He asked, "Now, what's that crap they got down there when people die? They gets up a big parade, follow the body to the graveyard. Every ass crying and moaning and groaning like the world's coming to an end. Then no sooner than they place the dead person in the grave all hell breaks out and everybody suddenly stops weeping and starts dancing, singing, screaming and raising all sorts of hell. How that originated?"

I shrugged my shoulders.

He continued, "You all are crazy down there. I once had a woman from down there. She was as pretty as a speckled pup but crazy as a loon. Go to church every day, cursed like a sailor, she believed that voodoo stuff. Burned all kinds of candles, red, black, green, white, brown, purple. I never knew candles came in all them colors. On the wall she tacked up pictures of St. Peter, St. John, St. Thomas, John the Baptist. She burned incense – I didn't know they had all them different saints.

"She was pretty and she was clean. She could cook better than that head chef at the Waldorf. She would cook up stuff, all kinds of vegetables, smelled good, looked good and tasted good. Every morning at seven o'clock she went to the Catholic Church. She said, 'I'm going to confess to the priest.'

"I did not like that because I am an underworld man. I was always very scared and I expected the dicks to grab me any time. She was crazy; her name was Estella and she was pretty as a peach. Then one morning she was packing her clothes. I asked her where she was going and she started to cry. She told me she dreamed that her mother was sick. 'I'm going to New Orleans,' she told me. "I'll be back in a couple of weeks."

"In a week I gets a special delivery letter. She wrote that she loved me but I was too wicked. She wrote that I was the devil. Later she sent me a medal. It was a saint and it had a silver chain so I could wear it around my neck for good luck. I do believe that medal was good luck because I had a streak of good luck for about a year. I hit the numbers every week. Won at the race track and won at dice games. Estella would write me a letter about every month and then I stopped hearing from her. I wrote and her brother answered my letter. He wrote that she had passed on. My luck changed. I went to jail – aw, let's talk about something else – come on, I'm buying everybody a drink".

He poured drinks for all. He looked over in the corner and yelled, "Green, git up and see, you might want to pee".

Green slowly opened his eyes and slowly let his eyeballs descend.

Charleston yelled, "Green, if you want this whisky git up off your behind and come and git." Two of the corner-sitters got up and slowly came to the table. The light caused their bloodshot eyes to squint.

Charleston announced, "So Green ain't moving. We will let him sit there until the *rigor mortis* sets in!"

Charleston lifted his glass to say a toast and a whisky voiced chorus slowly started to chant, watching Charleston's lips: "We will sit Big Green on the steps to catch some fresh air."

Index